mean cheap necessarily. Food lovers know the difference between a restaurant where the high prices are fully justified by the quality of the ingredients and the excellence of the cooking and presentation of the food, and meretricious establishments where high prices are merely the result of pretentious attitudes.

Some of the restaurants featured here are undeniably expensive if you consume caviar and champagne, but even haute cuisine establishments offer set-price menus (especially at lunchtime) allowing budget diners to enjoy dishes created by top chefs and every bit as good as those on the regular menu. At the same time, some of the eating places listed here might not make it into more conventional food guides, because they are relatively humble cafés or takeaways. Some are deliberately oriented towards tourists, but there is nothing wrong in that: what some guides dismiss as 'tourist traps' may be deservedly popular for providing choice and good value.

FEEDBACK

You may or may not agree with the author's choice – in either case we would like to know about your experiences. Any feedback you give us and any recommendations you make will be followed up, so that you can look forward to seeing your restaurant suggestions in print in the next edition.

Feedback forms have been included at the back of the book and you can e-mail us with comments by writing to: *timeforfood@thomascook.com*. No food guide can keep pace with the changing restaurant scene, as chefs move on, establishments open or close, and menus, opening hours or credit card details change. Let us know what you like or do not like about the restaurants featured here. Tell us if you discover shops, pubs, cafés, bars, restaurants or markets that

you think should go in the guide. Let us know if you discover changes – say to telephone numbers or opening times.

Symbols used in this guide

VISA	Visa accepted
◐	Diners Club accepted
MasterCard	MasterCard accepted
🍴	Restaurant
🍷	Bar, café or pub
🧺	Shop, market or picnic site
∅	Telephone
◉	Transport
❷	Numbered red circles relate to the maps at the start of the section

The price indications used in this guide have the following meanings:

❶	budget level
❶❶	typical/average for the destination
❶❶❶	up-market

FOOD FINDER

EUROPEAN
Bonsoir Clara 29

FRENCH
L'Alban Chambon 19
Armand & Ko 9
Atelier Européen 48, 57
ATM (à toi Mauricette) 79
The Avenue 59
Le Bison Teint 60
Bistrot du Mail 68
Brasseries Georges 68
Bruneau 56
Les Capucines 79
Le Cerf 9
Chez Callens 48
Chez Marius en Provence 38
Les Continents 49
L'Épicerie 10
Ma Folle de Soeur 79
Le Gourmandine 39
Grandeur Nature 80
L'Idiot du Village 39
Inada 81
Le Joueur de Flûte 40
Lola 40
Le Loup-Galant 31
La Maison du Boeuf 57, 61
La Maison de Cygne 10
O'comme 3 Pommes 69
De L'Ogenblik 10
Les Petits Oignons 40
Au Plaisir 50
La Quincaillerie 70
Saint-Boniface 61
Le Serpolet 51
Stanhope-Brighton 51, 57
Stirwen 51
La Table de l'Abbaye 71
La Tour d'y Voir 41
Trente Rue de la Paille 41
La Truffe Noire 57, 71
Villa Lorraine 57

FRENCH PROVENCAL
Bar Bar Sol 59

FUSION
Les Jardins de Bagatelle 60

INDIAN
La Porte des Indes 70

INTERNATIONAL
Adrienne 59

ITALIAN
Aux Anges 79
Al Piccolo Mondo 81
ATM (à toi Mauricette) 79
Chez Martin 19
Fellini 69
Ricotta & Parmesan 20
Roma 21
La Scala 61
La Truffe Noire 57, 71

JAPANESE
Samourai 21
Tagawa 71

LATIN AMERICAN
Tierra del Fuego 61

MEDITERRANEAN
Les Continents 49

PORTUGUESE
La Forcado 79

SEAFOOD
La Belle Maraichère 29, 37
Au Boeuf Gros Sel 37
L'Écailler du Palais Royal 38, 57
François 29, 37
L'Huîtrière 30
Le Jardin de Catherine 31
La Marée 19
La Moulière 37
Le Pre Salé 37
La Quincaillerie 70
Scheltema 37
Sea Grill 21, 57
La Tortue du Zoute 41
La Truit d'Argent 31
Au Vieux Bruxelles 37
Vimar 51

SPANISH
Le Jardin d'Espagne 49

THAI
Les Perles de Pluie 70
Phat Thai 19

TUNISIAN
Aux Mille et Une Nuits 81

VEGETARIAN
Grandeur Nature 80

VIETNAMESE
Les Baguetes Imperiales 57

OTHER
Les 4 Seasons 57
Atrium 57

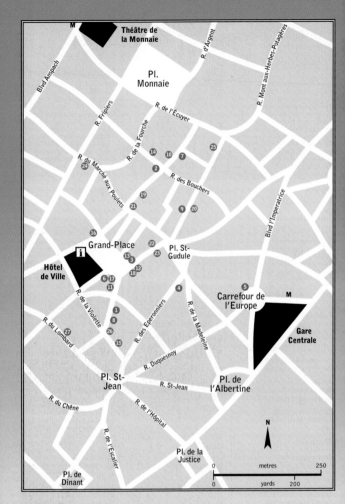

Around Grand-Place

This vibrant city centre district is abuzz with welcoming bistros and bars, popular restaurants and a host of appealing specialist shops. Classy Galeries Saint-Hubert is reputed to be the first covered shopping street in Europe, and the mouth-watering street names surrounding Grand-Place serve to remind us of the mercantile origins of the city.

AROUND GRAND-PLACE
Restaurants

Armand & Ko ❶

R. des Chapeliers 16

☎ 514 1763

🚌 Buses 34, 48, 95 and 96

Open: daily 1200–1430, 1900–2300

Reservations recommended

All credit cards accepted

French

€€

Tourists rub shoulders with businessmen and gourmands in this friendly, old bistro, housed on two levels of an adorable 17th-century townhouse, just a stone's throw from Grand-Place. Choose from such delights as asparagus soup, stuffed courgette flowers, duck and prune terrine, roast beef stuffed with spinach and Niçoise salad from the daily menu, chalked up on the blackboard.

Aux Armes de Bruxelles ❷

R. des Bouchers 13

☎ 511 5598

🚇 Metro Bourse or trams 23, 52, 55, 56, 81 and 90

Open: Tue–Sun 1200–2315

Reservations recommended

All credit cards accepted

Belgian

€€

Aux Armes de Bruxelles is one of the best seafood restaurants in this street – a veritable Bruxellois institution, thanks to its tasteful, traditional décor, its swift, impeccable service, and tasty Belgian cuisine. The menu is vast, and includes mussels with chips, *waterzooi* (chicken cooked with cream and vegetables), shrimp croquettes and beef *carbonnade* (a flemish beef stew with onions and herbs braised in beer).

Le Cerf ❸

Grand-Place 20

☎ 511 4791

🚇 Metro Bourse or trams 23, 52, 55, 56, 81 and 90

Open: Mon, Tue, Thu–Sat 1800–2330, Wed 1200–1500, 1900–2330

Reservations recommended

All credit cards accepted

Belgian-French

€€€

Stepping inside this small, cosy restaurant, in a magnificent 17th-century mansion on the corner of Grand-Place, is like winding back the clocks to bygone days, with its ancient, rustic atmosphere, wood panelling, rich red fleur-de-lys fabrics and classical

▲ La Maison de Cygne

background music. The food is also traditional, full of strong, earthy flavours, with an appealing wine list to match.

L'Éperon d'Or ❹

R. des Eperonniers 8

✆ 512 5293

🅜 Buses 34, 48, 95 and 96

Open: Mon–Fri 1200–1430, 1900–2200

Reservations recommended

All credit cards accepted

Belgian

❷❷

For a taste of authentic Belgian cuisine in an ancient Bruxellois setting, book a table at 'The Golden Spur', and you won't be disappointed. For here in a quaint, dark dining room with just thirty covers, you will be able to taste the freshest of Zebrugge sole, thick slices of juicy Ardennes ham, veal kidneys in Leffe beer and fish *waterzooi*.

L'Épicerie ❺

Le Meridian, Carrefour de l'Europe

✆ 548 4716

🅜 Metro Gare Centrale or buses 29, 38, 60, 63, 65, 66 and 71

Open: daily 0700–1030, 1200–1445, 1900–2230, closed Sat lunch

Reservations recommended

All credit cards accepted

French

❸❸❸

Come here with an empty stomach and a full wallet! Young, French-born chef David Martin cooks predominantly French cuisine, using the freshest of Belgian produce. Choose from a variety of menus and relish such exquisite dishes as red mullet and almonds with fresh coriander and a coulis of avocado and lemon peel, followed by John Dory in a light Thai curry with ravioli of green apples and mint.

La Maison de Cygne ❻

Grand-Place 9 (entrance at r. Charles Buls 2)

✆ 511 8244

🅜 Metro Bourse or buses 34, 48, 95 and 96

Open: 1230–1400, 1915–2200, closed Sat lunch and Sun

Reservations not allowed

All credit cards accepted

French

❸❸❸

Before you go inside, note the unusual façade of this establishment; it was inspired by the Louis XIV style, and differs radically from the Flemish baroque style which predominates in the square. During the 18th century 'The House of the Swan' became the Butchers' Guildhall, then more recently it became Karl Marx's locale. At lunchtime it is crowded with businessmen tucking into truffles, *foie gras* and oysters with champagne. In the evening a more relaxed yet equally luxurious ambience makes it the ideal venue for that special occasion.

De L'Ogenblik ❼

Galerie des Princes 1

✆ 511 6151

🅜 Metro Gare Centrale or buses 29, 38, 60, 63, 65, 66 and 71

Open: 1200–1430, 1900–2400 (Fri–Sat 1900–2430), closed Sun

Reservations recommended

All credit cards accepted

French

❷❷

It's hard to beat 'At the Blink of an Eye' for its chic location, tasty

French cuisine, friendly service, young, arty crowd, and lively atmosphere. The menu varies daily according to the best market buys and typically includes tomato and fresh goats' cheese *bavarois* on a bed of fennel, roast pigeon in truffle juice, and a *millefeuille* of salmon, lobster and shrimp.

La Roue d'Or ⑧

R. des Chapeliers 26

Ø 514 2554

🚊 Buses 34, 48, 95 and 96

Open: daily 1200–2430

Reservations recommended

All credit cards accepted

Belgian

€€

This popular, 19th-century brasserie serves generous portions of Belgian regional cuisine in classic surrounds – mirrors and Magritte-style murals on the walls. The *plat du jour* is always a bargain. Alternatively try the smoked salmon and endive salad, the cuckoo *waterzooi*, or a T-bone steak.

La Taverne du Passage ⑨

Galerie de la Reine 30

Ø 512 3731

🚊 Metro Gare Centrale or buses 29, 38, 60, 63, 65, 66 and 71

Open: daily 1200–2400, closed Wed and Thu during June and July only

Reservations recommended

All credit cards accepted

Belgian

€€

Located under the soaring glass arcades of the Galeries Saint-Hubert, this classical, old-style restaurant, founded in 1928, is famous for its traditional Bruxellois cuisine. The interior is uninspiring, so take a table in the arcade instead, and watch the shoppers go by.

Vincent ⑩

R. des Dominicains 8–10

Ø 511 2607

🚊 Metro Bourse or trams 23, 52, 55, 56, 81 and 90

Open: daily 1200–1445, 1830–2330 (2200 on Sun)

Reservations not allowed

All credit cards accepted

Belgian

€€

You enter this restaurant through the kitchens, into the cheerful seating area, decorated with original 1912 tiled scenes of fishermen and oyster farmers, and even an ancient tiled menu serving roast beef at a mere 0.50BF. It goes without saying that the fish dishes here are exceptional, but the restaurant is equally known as a steakhouse.

▲ Tiled wall panel at Vincent

AROUND GRAND-PLACE
Bars, cafés and pubs

L'Auberge des Chapeliers ⓫

R. des Chapeliers 1–3

✆ 513 7338

Buses 34, 48, 95 and 96

Open: daily 1200–1400, 1830–2300 (Fri–Sat 2400)

All credit cards accepted

€

This long-established inn, just south of Grand-Place, is housed in a rickety old 17th-century building, formerly the Guildhall of Milliners (*Chapeliers*). Rustic and welcoming, it serves some of the best no-frills Belgian fare in town.

Barock's Café ⓬

Grand-Place 15

✆ 542 4198

Metro Bourse or buses 34, 48, 95 and 96

Open: 1100–2400

All credit cards accepted

€€

The perfect choice of venue when you can't decide whether to go for a drink or a meal. Here you'll find good beer *and* a splendid menu of Belgian fare. The décor gibes at baroque art (hence the name), with its modern 'Breughelian' scenes, and ceiling painted with 21st-century angels floating on clouds.

La Chaloupe d'Or ⓭

Grand-Place 24–5

✆ 511 4161

Metro Bourse or buses 34, 48, 95 and 96

Open: daily 0900–0100 (Fri–Sat 0200)

VISA, MasterCard

€€

This celebrated bar, previously home to the Tailor's Guildhall, now grandly entitled 'The Golden Sloop', is popular with both locals and tourists. Its location, overlooking the daily flower market on Grand-Place, makes it an ideal venue to while away a few hours sipping cocktails.

▲ t'Kelderke

Léon ⓮

R. des Bouchers 18

✆ 511 1415

Metro Bourse or trams 23, 52, 55, 56, 81 and 90

Open: daily 1200–2300 (Fri–Sat 2330)

All credit cards accepted

€€

Founded in 1893 and perhaps the most renowned of all Belgian *moules-frites* restaurants, this is the original of the great Léon chain, huge and multi-storeyed but always crowded, with paper tablecloths, fast service and enormous pots of steaming mussels prepared in a variety of different ways.

Maison du Valais 'Son Carnotzet' ⓯

R. de la Violette 32

✆ 511 9767

Buses 34, 48, 95 and 96

Open: 1200–1400, 1900–2300, closed Sat lunch and Mon lunch

VISA, MasterCard

€€

Step inside the Maison du Valais and you'd be forgiven for thinking you were in a Swiss mountain chalet, with

its pine interior, its red-and-white checked tablecloths and its alpine feel. Order the gruyère quiche, veal sausages with *rösti*, or a meat or cheese fondue to complete the scene.

Le Roi d'Espagne

Grand-Place 1

✆ 513 0807

Ⓜ Metro Bourse or buses 34, 48, 95 and 96

Open: daily 1000–0100

All credit cards accepted

ⓔ ⓔ

This magnificent building was once the Guildhall of Bakers, hence the allegorical statues of Energy, Fire, Wind, Water, Wheat and Prudence balanced on the balustrade – all the necessary elements for baking perfect bread. The bar is always full, as is the terrace in summer. Enjoy the barrelled beers, the hearty Bruxellois menu and the views over Grand-Place.

La Rose Blanche

Grand-Place 11

✆ 513 6479

Ⓜ Metro Bourse or buses 34, 48, 95 and 96

Open: daily 1000–0200

All credit cards accepted

ⓔ ⓔ

'The White Rose' with its exposed beams and original 17th-century stucco rose motifs, makes an ideal lunch stop. They say French novelist Victor Hugo lived here for a year. He too would probably

have enjoyed the nourishing chicken in Kriek beer, the fricassee of frogs' legs and the mussels served here today, plus the extensive selection of beers.

t'Kelderke ⓲

Grand-Place 15

✆ 513 7344

Ⓜ Metro Bourse or buses 34, 48, 95 and 96

Open: daily 1200–0200

All credit cards accepted

ⓔ ⓔ

In this 17th-century vaulted cellar tuck into hearty Belgian dishes – *bloedpans* (black tripe), mussels *au gratin*, and *waterzooi* at surprisingly reasonable prices. Robust beers and wines complement the cuisine, including t'Kelderke, their very own beer, served in 1.5-, 4.5-, or 6.9-litre magnums.

Toone

Impasse Schuddeveld 6, petit rue des Bouchers

✆ 513 5486

Ⓜ Metro Bourse or trams 23, 52, 55, 56, 81 and 90

Open: daily 1200–2400

No credit cards accepted

ⓔ

This small, weather-beaten bar, attached to a tiny puppet theatre, has been popular for over 170 years, with its reasonably priced beer list and a modest choice of sandwiches and snacks. It's difficult to find, but worth hunting out for its tiny, peaceful courtyard.

La Vache qui regarde passer les trains ⓴

Galerie de la Reine 29

✆ 513 3336

Ⓜ Metro Gare Centrale or buses 29, 38, 60, 63, 65, 66 and 71

Open: daily 0800–1000

All credit cards accepted

ⓔ

This friendly café, in the sumptuous Galeries Saint-Hubert, is decked out in bare brick and cream tiles, giving it a fashionable 'dairy' feel. All day it serves shoppers a healthy selection of sandwiches, salads, homemade soups, quiches, yoghurts, patisseries and ice creams, together with teas, coffees, milkshakes and a tempting weekend brunch (*1030–1500*).

AROUND GRAND-PLACE
Shops, markets and picnic sites

Shops

Bier Tempel 21

R. Marché aux Herbes 56

Metro Bourse or trams 23, 52, 55, 56, 81 and 90

Open: daily 1000–1900

All credit cards accepted

Welcome to beer heaven! This shop is an absolute must for drinkers of fine ales, with its impressive selection of Belgian beers, together with all the corresponding glasses, including special tulip-shaped ones for La Chouffe, wineglass-shaped ones for De Koninck, and even the unusual Kwak beer glasses, shaped like an hourglass, and held within a wooden stand. Or how about some beer jelly to spread on bread or pancakes, or to make into beer sauce for meats?

▲ La Boutique Tintin

La Boutique Tintin 22

R. de la Colline 13

Metro Bourse or trams 23, 52, 55, 56, 81 and 90

Open: Mon 1100–1800, Tue–Sat 1000–1800, Sun 1100–1700

All credit cards accepted

With Brussels as Europe's cartoon-strip capital, no visit would be complete without a visit to the official Tintin shop where, together with posters, T-shirts and other memorabilia, you will find a delightful selection of teacups, teapots, trays, plates and bowls featuring Tintin, Snowy, Captain Haddock et al.

Brussels Pralines 23

R. de la Colline 4

Metro Bourse and trams 23, 52, 55, 56, 81 and 90

Open: daily 0930–2130

All credit cards accepted

Forget all the handmade, too-good-to-eat designer Belgian pralines of Godiva and Neuhaus! This specialist chocolate shop serves much more down-to-earth creations which make great gifts – chocolate cars, planes, teddies, crocodiles, beer bottles … even chocolate versions of the city's best-loved fountain of a small boy having a wee

– the celebrated Mannekin Pis.

Café-Tasse Store 24

R. Marché aux Herbes 15

Metro Bourse or trams 23, 52, 55, 56, 81 and 90

Open: Mon–Sat 0900–1800 (Fri–Sat 1830)

All credit cards accepted

This bright, sunshine-coloured shop, with its country-style pine fittings, specialises in coffees, teas and chocolate products, including chocolate-coated coffee beans from six different countries. Upstairs is a small café area serving a selection of coffees and scrumptious hot chocolates, with chunky slices of *pain d'épices* (spiced fruit loaf) and chocolate brownies.

Corné Food & Corné Toison d'Or 25

Galerie du Roi 24–6

Metro Gare Centrale or buses 29, 38, 60, 63, 65, 66 and 71

Open: Mon–Sat 1000–1900, Sun 1030–1830

All credit cards accepted

The speciality of this traditional confectionery shop is the *manon*, a large round chocolate filled with fresh cream. But don't stop there! Try the florentines, the crystalised fruits, the jams, the waffles, the spiced breads, the specialist teas and coffees, the handmade truffles and pralines …

Dragées Marechal 26

R. des Chapeliers 40

Buses 34, 48, 95 and 96

Open: Tue–Sun 1000–1800

No credit cards accepted

As the name suggests, this old-fashioned corner sweet-shop, founded in 1848, specialises in sugared almonds (*dragées*), gift-wrapped in fancy gift boxes and exquisite porcelain containers, and given traditionally in Belgium to guests at christenings.

Godiva 3

Grand-Place 21

Metro Bourse or trams 23, 52, 55, 56, 81 and 90

Open: Mon–Sat 0900–2200, Sun 1000–2200

All credit cards accepted

Godiva is the world leader in luxury confectionery. Manufactured to the original recipes and employing traditional methods, these handmade chocolates are every chocoholic's dream.

Neuhaus 13

Galerie de la Reine

Gare Centrale or buses 29, 38, 60, 63, 65, 66 and 71

Open: Mon–Sat 1000–2000, Sun 1000–1900

All credit cards accepted

Located in a prime position within the

▲ Rue des Bouchers

Galeries Saint-Hubert, this late 19th-century shop is one the most beautiful of Brussels' many Neuhaus branches. Choose from row upon row of gleaming handmade chocolates on display, including chocolate-covered caramels, pralines, *manons* and liqueur-filled ones, or simply opt for a simple chocolate bar in a variety of flavours or, in summer months, an ice cream from the barrow outside.

Planète Chocolat 27

R. du Lombard 24

Buses 34, 48, 95 and 96

Open: Tue–Sat 1000–1830, Sun 1500–2100

All credit cards accepted

Once dubbed the 'Willy-Wonka of Brussels', expert chocolate-maker Frank Duval believes 'few people understand the true spirit of chocolate – it is an art-form', and he is eager to teach us. His dazzling orange shop

therefore not only sells his moreish creations, but also offers informative displays on chocolate manufacture, artisan equipment, tastings (there's a tearoom at the back) and chocolate-making demonstrations (most Saturdays at 1500).

Rubbrecht 3

Grand-Place 23

Metro Bourse or trams 23, 52, 55, 56, 81 and 90

Open: Mon–Sat 0900–1900, Sun 1000–1800

All credit cards accepted

Belgium has long been famous for the finest lace in the world. Sadly, today few local people learn the craft and as a consequence, genuine handmade lace is pricey and very much in demand. Here, at Brussels' top lace shop, you can find a wonderful choice of pretty, handmade lace table-pieces, all genuinely Belgian, and some antique, to grace any dinner table.

Belgian beers

Individualistic brews

Blond beer, wheat beer, amber beer, dark beer, fruit beer, Trappist and Lambic beer, Kriek, Gueuze and Faro … there's no denying Belgium is a beer connoisseur's heaven, with over 400 different varieties, each unique and suited to a particular taste and occasion. As Michael Jackson remarked in *The Great Beers of Belgium*: 'No country can match Belgium in the gastronomic interest of its beers. No country has so many distinct styles of beer. No country has beers that are so complex in character. No country has so many individualistic brews … The respect reserved for wine in most countries is in Belgium accorded to beer.'

Beer drinking in Belgium is something of a ritual. Each beer has certain criteria: the best temperature, the correct method of pouring it, and many come with their own glass, specially designed to optimise the liquid's fragrance and flavour. Order a

'lunette' in **Café La Lunette** (*pl. de la Monnaie; ∅ 218 0378; open: daily 0800–0100*) and your beer will be served in a one-litre *coupe* (an outsized wineglass); try a 'kwak' at **Le Roi d'Espagne** in Grand-Place (*see page 13*), and you will be expected to leave a shoe as a deposit for the unusual hourglass-shaped glass, held upright in a wooden stand, to stop you running off with it as a souvenir!

Beer is very much the national drink, with Belgians consuming an average 120 litres of beer per head annually. But it's not always obvious that they're drinking beer. If you see a champagne bottle being uncorked and sparkling pink liquid being poured into a flute, don't assume it's pink champagne! More likely it's **Framboise**, a sweet-tasting Lambic beer aperitif, flavoured with raspberries. The wineglass, full of claret-coloured liquid? It's probably **Rodenback**, an oak-aged beer – the perfect accompaniment to a rich, meaty stew. And the brandy snifter? That's almost certainly a rich, chocolatey *digestif* beer, produced at a Trappist monastery, and akin to a bottle-aged port.

Such is the astonishing variety of beers, when you go into a bar you'll probably be given a menu – not for the food but for the beer. There are several specialist beer bars in Brussels.

The most famous is **Moeder Lambic** (*see page 83*), a small, unassuming bar at the heart of Saint-Gilles which claims to stock over a thousand different bottled beers. To help you through their extensive menu, you'll find some essential 'beer vocabulary' on pages 90–3 of this book. Remember Belgian beer is not for those on a booze run, but rather it should be savoured like a fine wine. Be sure to taste some typically Bruxellois beers such as **Gueuze, Faro** and **Kriek**. Don't knock them back in a hurry, watch their strength – some contain up to 12 per cent alcoholic content – and be warned, the rarer the beer, the higher the price!

To learn some of the secrets of Belgium's age-old beer tradition, the **Brewery Museum** (*Grand-Place 10; ∅ 511 4987; open: daily 1000–1700*) is appropriately located in the former guildhall of the once powerful Corporation of Brewers. What's more, afterwards, you are ideally placed for some serious tasting on one of the outdoor terraces in Grand-Place (*see pages 12–13*). To learn about unique Lambic beer, a spontaneously fermented beer and Brussels' pride-and-joy, visit the **Cantillon Brewery** (*r. Gheude 56; ∅ 521 4928; ◉ metro Gare du Midi or Clemenceau; open: Mon-Fri 0830–1700, Sat 1000–1700*), a hundred-year-old family-run

firm, proud of its strictly traditional methods and antique brewing equipment. It brews just 700,000 litres a year and bills itself as a 'living brewery museum'. The entrance fee entitles you to a glass of Gueuze (pronounced 'gurrs'), a naturally sparkling blend of old and new lambics.

To stock up on beer to take home, connoisseurs should visit specialist shops **Bier Tempel** (*see page 14*) and **Beer Mania** (*see page 65*), both with a dazzling choice of brews together with their corresponding glasses. Sometimes they have in stock such special beers as limited-edition Millennium Gueuze, various Christmas beverages, or Gouden Carolus's 'Cuvée of the Emperor', brewed once a year in limited quantity on 24 February, in honour of King Charles V's birthday. Ordinary grocers and supermarkets in the suburbs usually have a good selection, and at reasonable prices too.

> **Beer is very much the national drink, with Belgians consuming an average 120 litres of beer per head annually.**

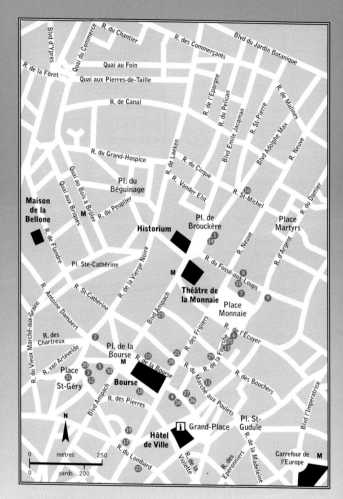

The City Centre

The city centre presents a slice of real, everyday Brussels where elegant belle-époque cafés and brasseries rub shoulders with minimalist shops and neon-lit fast-food joints. Immediately west of Grand-Place a host of enticing little gourmet shops can be found, while place Saint-Géry is one of the trendiest spots in town, humming with cafés and bars.

THE CITY CENTRE
Restaurants

L'Alban Chambon ❶

Hôtel Metropole, pl. de Brouckère 31

∅ 217 2300

Ⓜ Metro De Brouckère or trams 23, 52, 55, 56, 81 and 90

Open: Mon–Fri 1200–1430, 1900–2230

Reservations recommended

All credit cards accepted

French

❸❸❸

Here you can enjoy the finest of French cuisine in the luxurious surroundings of a grand belle-époque salon. Order the house specialities – petals of potatoes, served with truffles and langoustines roasted in lemon juice, followed by scallops in truffle vinaigrette – and you will be assured a meal to remember.

La Bourse ❷

R. Auguste Ort 31

∅ 511 9929

Ⓜ Metro Bourse or trams 23, 52, 55, 56, 81 and 90

Open: daily 1100–2400

Reservations unnecessary

Belgian

❸❸

There's always a lively, fun atmosphere in this simple, psychedelic-orange café. Try the beef *carbonnade*, the frogs' legs, a steaming pot of *moules-frites* – or, if you're starving hungry, the sauerkraut served with a huge knuckle of ham.

Chez Martin ❸

R. Borgval 15

∅ 513 9303

Ⓜ Metro Bourse or trams 23, 52, 55, 56, 81 and 90

Open: daily 1900–2300

Reservations recommended

No credit cards accepted

Italian

❸❸

The restaurant is run by a mother and son, and their welcoming manner and friendly service makes you feel almost part of the family. Start with the mixed vegetable *antipasti* platter – a colourful array of peppers, aubergines, tomatoes and courgettes roasted in a nutty olive oil – then move on to the *tagliatelle au scampi* or the ravioli filled with four cheeses. No Bruxellois menu would be complete without the ubiquitous *dame blanche* (vanilla ice cream with hot Belgian chocolate sauce) for dessert.

La Marée ❹

R. au Beurre 19

∅ 502 9055

Ⓜ Metro Bourse or trams 23, 52, 55, 56, 81 and 90

Open: daily 1100–2400

Reservations recommended

All credit cards accepted

Seafood

❸❸

Ask for a table on the pint-sized pavement terrace, so that you can watch the world go by whilst tucking into an enormous shellfish platter – a spectacular array of oysters, mussels, cockles, whelks, sea snails, crab and giant prawns. The menu also includes paella, *bouillabaisse*, *moules au gratin* and simply grilled cod, monkfish and salmon, together with a smattering of dishes for non-fish eaters.

Phat Thai ❺

R. Jules Van Praet 32

∅ 511 8243

Ⓜ Metro Bourse or trams 23, 52, 55, 56, 81 and 90

Open: 1200–1500, 1800–0200, closed Sun lunch and Tue

Reservations recommended

All credit cards accepted

Thai

❸❸

In summer, Phat Thai's tables spill out on to the pavement, luring passers-by with its fragrant cuisine: prawn soup with lemongrass

and coconut milk,
chicken baked in
banana leaves, fried
pork with chilli and a
Thai spices, duck in a
spicy red curry sauce ...
the choice is endless.

Ricotta & Parmesan ⑥

R. de l'Écuyer 31

✆ 502 8082	
ⓜ Metro De Brouckère or trams 23, 52, 55, 56, 81 and 90	
Open: 1130–1500, 1900–0200, closed Sat lunch and Sun	
Reservations recommended	
All credit cards accepted	
Italian	
€ €	

The restaurant's two
young patrons have
concocted some delicate
but original dishes
including broad bean
and *pancetta* salad with
a seven herb dressing;
courgettes stuffed with
mozzarella, tomatoes
and basil; and *ziti* (a
type of pasta) with
Parma ham and wild

mushrooms – all washed down with New World wines.

Roma

R. des Princes 12–14

✆ 219 0194

Ⓜ Metro De Brouckère or trams 23, 52, 55, 56, 81 and 90

Open: 1200–1500, 1900–2330, closed Sat lunch and Sun

Reservations recommended

All credit cards accepted

Italian

€€€

One of Brussels' leading Italian restaurants, conveniently located beside the **Théâtre de la Monnaie** and especially popular after performances. Dine on carpaccio with truffle oil, seafood risotto, lamb stuffed with ricotta and mascarpone, *saltimbocca* (veal wrapped in Parma ham with fresh sage) and the lightest, creamiest tiramisu imaginable.

Samourai ⑧

R. du Fossé-aux-Loups 28

✆ 217 5639

Ⓜ Metro De Brouckère or trams 23, 52, 55, 56, 81 and 90

Open: 1200–1400, 1900–2200, closed Sun lunch and Tue

Reservations essential

All credit cards accepted

Japanese

€€

This exclusive restaurant is an absolute gem. The tiny interior is minimalist yet typically Japanese and the cooking is truly authentic. House specialities include sushi, *sashimi* and *tempura*, exquisitely presented in hand-crafted pottery. For the more adventurous, try one of the *dégustation* (tasting) menus.

Sea Grill ⑨

Hotel Radisson, r. du Fossé-aux-Loups

✆ 227 3120

Ⓜ Metro De Brouckère or trams 23, 52, 55, 56, 81 and 90

Open: 1200–1430, 1900–2230, closed Sat lunch and Sun

Reservations recommended at weekends

All credit cards accepted

Seafood

€€€

At this top fish restaurant fish tanks, seashells and large glass wall panels depicting a Scandinavian fjord landscape help to get you in the mood. Specialities include Norwegian smoked salmon *gravlaks*, whole sea bass cooked in a coarse sea salt crust and pressed Brittany lobster, prepared at the table.

Tassili ⑩

R. du Fossé-aux-Loups 11

✆ 219 1568

Ⓜ Metro De Brouckère and trams 23, 52, 55, 56, 81 and 90

Open: daily 1130–1500, 1830–0100

Reservations recommended

▭▭ ▭▭

Algerian

€€

You'll find an unusual choice of fragrant Algerian dishes here, together with all the usual North African favourites – *chak-choukha* (a piquant ratatouille with *harissa*, egg and spiced meat), *tagines* (meat and vegetable stews), couscous and grilled meats. The setting is elegant, with Moorish décor and tables lit by small coloured lamps. Some weekends there's belly dancing!

THE CITY CENTRE
Bars, cafés and pubs

Le Bar à Tapas

R. Borgval 11

✆ 502 6602

🚇 Metro Bourse or trams 23, 52, 55, 56, 81 and 90

Open: Mon–Thu 1730–0100, Fri–Sun 1730–0230

The shabby exterior of this Spanish-style bar belies a warm and exotic interior, with subdued lighting, comfortable chairs and salsa music. The various *tapas* dishes are reasonably priced and contain all the usual favourites – *chorizo*, prawns in garlic, mushrooms, squid, snails, anchovies, tortilla ... and an extensive choice of sherries and cocktails.

À la Becasse

R. de Tabora 11

✆ 511 0006

🚇 Metro Bourse or trams 23, 52, 55, 56, 81 and 90

Open: Mon–Thu 1100–0100, Fri–Sat 1100–0200, Sun 1100–2400

For over a hundred years, this jolly beer hall has been something of a Bruxellois institution, where beer (in earthenware jugs) flows by the litre, accompanied either by sensational sandwiches or a delicious steak tartare, the perfect pick-me-up following a heavy night out on the town.

Au Bon Vieux Temps ⑪

Impasse St-Nicolas, r. du Marché aux Herbes 12

✆ 217 2626

🚇 Metro Bourse or trams 23, 52, 55, 56, 81 and 90

Open: daily 1100–2430

No credit cards accepted

Hidden down an alleyway near Grand-Place, this 17th-century tavern has managed to preserve the atmosphere of bygone days, thanks to its extensive wood panelling, its cosy nooks and crannies, and an old-fashioned fireplace. Enjoy a drink at the bar or at one of the ancient tile-inlaid tables – there's a good choice of popular beers on offer.

Café Metropole ⑭

Hôtel Metropole, pl. de Brouckère 31

✆ 219 2384

🚇 Metro De Brouckère or trams 23, 52, 55, 56, 81 and 90

Open: daily 0900–2400

All credit cards accepted

This *fin-de-siècle* café, with its glamorous leather and wood interior, candelabras, stained-glass windows and a broad pavement terrace, was famous during the *belle époque* as the place to see and be seen in Brussels. Unfortunately, today it rests on its laurels: service is unfriendly and prices are high but, nonetheless, it remains popular.

Le Cirio ⑮

R. de la Bourse 18–20

✆ 512 1395

🚇 Metro Bourse or trams 23, 52, 55, 56, 81 and 90

Open: daily 1000–0100

No credit cards accepted

Once a favourite haunt of Jacques Brel, this magnificent old bar-cum-brasserie alongside the Belgian Stock Exchange is renowned for its 'half-en-half' (a heady mix of champagne and white wine), a drink created here many decades ago and still *the* thing to order.

Le Corbeau 16

R. St-Michel 18–20

∅ 219 5246

🚇 Metro De Brouckère or trams 23, 52, 55, 56, 81 and 90

Open: Mon–Thu 0930–2400, Fri–Sat 0930–0400

No credit cards accepted

🅒

'The Raven' bar is surprisingly quiet by day, but makes up for it during the evenings, as one of the wilder watering-holes in central Brussels. At weekends, a DJ plays all the latest sounds, the young, lively student crowds spill out on to the pavement and, once the floor space is all taken, table-dancing becomes the order of the day.

Dolores 17

R. Marché au Charbon

∅ 0476 530 499 (mobile)

🚌 Buses 34, 48, 95 and 96

Open: Fri–Wed 1200–2300

No credit cards accepted

🅒

This small, bright orange café is a popular spot to

while away the hours over a jug of homemade sangria, or to tuck into a big bowl of chilli or some authentic *tapas*. What's more, there's always a friendly welcome and foot-tapping Spanish music.

Le Falstaff 18

R. Henri Maus 45

∅ 512 1761

🚇 Metro Bourse or trams 23, 52, 55, 56, 81 and 90

Open: daily 1200–1500, 1830–2330

All credit cards accepted

🅒🅒

Another stunning art-nouveau brasserie near the Stock Exchange, dating from 1883, which draws locals and tourists alike here for its good-value Belgian cuisine. Try the rabbit and beer casserole, the sauerkraut or the beef *carbonnade*, then sit back on the terrace (heated in winter) and watch the Bruxellois go by.

H²O 19

R. Marché au Charbon 27

∅ 512 3843

🚌 Buses 34, 48, 95 and 96

Open: daily 1900–0200

No credit cards accepted

🅒🅒

This small, eccentric bistro, with Tolkien-style fantasy sculptures, aquamarine walls, candles and classical music, is especially popular with both couples and gays. The menu is simple – salads and tagliatelle – with some unusual flavour combinations.

Zebra Bar 20

Pl. St-Géry 33–5

∅ 511 0901

🚇 Metro Bourse or trams 23, 52, 55, 56, 81 and 90

Open: daily 0730–0200

No credit cards accepted

🅒

One of a handful of *in* bars in place Saint-Géry, Zebra Bar's terrace has a chic, upbeat nature, excellent cocktails, bar snacks and a sunny terrace – ideally positioned for people-watching.

THE CITY CENTRE
Shops, markets and picnic sites

Shops

Crousty ㉑

R. des Fripiers 2

🚇 Metro De Brouckère or trams 23, 52, 55, 56, 81 and 90

Open: Mon–Fri 0500–1900, Sat–Sun 0400–1900

No credit cards accepted

Along with bread baked in traditional wood-ovens, this bakery and patisserie sells a luscious selection of tarts, gateaux, croissants, quiches and crusty French sticks with a variety of fillings. There are a few tables too for breakfast, lunch and tea.

Dans la Presse ce Jour–là ㉒

R. du Lombard 23

🚌 Buses 34, 48, 95 and 96

Open: Mon–Fri 1130–1830, Sat 1130–1700

💳 American Express

Instead of the usual bouquet of flowers or a box of chocolates to celebrate a birthday, why not buy a loved one a bottle of port, wine or armagnac produced in the year of their birth at this highly specialised shop. They also sell Belgian, French, Dutch and British newspapers dating back as far as 1895 (hence the name of the shop, 'In the Press that Day').

Les Délices de Melanie ㉓

R. Grétry 27

🚇 Metro De Brouckère or trams 23, 52, 55, 56, 81 and 90

Open: Mon–Wed 1030–1830, Thu and Sat 1030–1900, Fri 1030–1930

All credit cards accepted

An old-fashioned chocolate shop, specialising in pralines and truffles, deliciously arranged in heart-shaped boxes. Ideal for St Valentine's Day!

Dandoy ㉔

R. au Beurre 31

🚇 Metro Bourse or trams 23, 52, 55, 61, 81 and 90

Open: Mon–Sat 0830–1830,
Sun 1030–1830

All credit cards accepted

The city's most famous
bakery, founded in
1829, sells traditional
Bruxellois fare including
speculoos (caramelised
biscuits baked in
wooden moulds), *pain à
la Greque* (spiced bread)
and *frangipanes*
(almond-flavoured
cakes), not to mention
the best marzipan in
Belgium. The entire
shop smells of almonds,
butter and cinnamon,
but the window displays
alone make your mouth
water!

Les Fromages Langhendries 25

R. de la Fourche 41

Metro De Brouckère or
trams 23, 52, 55, 56, 81
and 90

Open: Tue–Sat 0915–1815

No credit cards accepted

The cheese specialist of
central Brussels. You'll
find a staggering choice
of cheeses from all over
Europe here, including
almost every type of
cheese made in Belgium.

Galler 26

R. au Beurre 44

Metro Bourse or trams
23, 52, 55, 56, 81 and 90

Open: daily 1000–2130

All credit cards accepted

If it's good enough for
the King of Belgium, it
must be good enough
for us! Galler holds the
Royal Warrant for
chocolate-making
and, as a result, is

world-famous for its
handmade chocolates,
cocoa powder, praline-
filled waffles and its
unique chocolate
langues de chat (cats'
tongues).

Oliviers & Co 27

R. au Beurre 28

Metro Bourse or trams
23, 52, 55, 56, 81 and 90

Open: daily 0900–2100

American Express

The only specialist oil
shop in town, with an
excellent range of
smartly displayed bot-
tles, jars and canisters
containing oils, vine-
gars, tapenades, olives
and pestos, mostly from
France and Italy. There's
a small tasting area at
the back of the shop.

Le P'tit Normand 28

R. de Tabora 5

Open: Mon–Sat 0900–1830

Metro Bourse or trams
23, 52, 55, 56, 81 and 90

No credit cards accepted

This small *charcuterie*
shop is dominated by a
massive counter,
crammed with hams,
pâtés and cold cuts,
while a varied assort-
ment of sausages and
salamis hang from the
rafters. Try the *saucis-
son de Florenville* – it
contains Orval beer.
There's a **P'tit Normand
cheese shop** across the
road (*Tabora 8*), but the
service is not always
helpful or polite.

Simonis 29

R. Grétry 73

Metro De Brouckère or
trams 23, 52, 55, 56, 81
and 90

Open: daily 1000–1830

All credit cards accepted

This vintner has a good
selection of French
wines, a smattering of
bottles from the rest of
the world, plenty of
spirits and a large
choice of flavoured *gen-
ever* (Belgian gin).

Au Suisse 30

Blvd Anspach 73–5

Metro Bourse or trams
23, 52, 55, 56 and 81

Open: Mon–Sat 0830–1900

No credit cards accepted

A Brussels institution
since 1876, and *the*
place to buy your sand-
wiches, with counters
for salad, cheese, cold
meats and other fillings,
and a separate counter
for hot and cold drinks,
including homemade
milkshakes and freshly
squeezed fruit juices.

Sushi Factory 31

Pl. St-Géry 28

Metro Bourse or trams
23, 52, 55, 56, 81 and 90

Open: daily 1100–1430,
1630–2130

Tokyo meets Brussels at
this modern takeaway
sushi bar on the corner
of fashionable place
Saint-Géry. Choose from
a selection of individual
items or pick up a *bento*
– a ready-packed lunch-
box full of sushi.

Stoemp and chips

Potatophilia

According to Ruth Van Waerebeek, author of the best-selling *Everybody Eats Well in Belgium Cookbook*, 'Belgium is a nation of potatophiles ... What pasta is to Italy, the potato is to Belgium'. Whether they're baked, boiled, mashed, roasted, stuffed, gratinéed or fried, they are a staple of every Belgian meal. They can even make up the entire meal. Two particular potato dishes (Belgian versions of universal favourites) warrant special mention – *stoemp* and chips.

Stoemp is the ultimate in Belgian comfort food. It's a homely, uncomplicated, country dish, deeply rooted in the Belgian tradition of peasant cooking, but unusual in that there is no one fixed recipe. Essentially it is a hearty mixture of mashed potatoes and cooked vegetables (usually whatever's in season, or left over from a previous meal), sometimes enriched with butter or cream and bacon, and seasoned with fresh herbs and spices (frequently nutmeg). You'll find *stoemp* on every traditional Bruxellois menu. Some of the best *stoemp* concoctions are served at the famous old brasserie **Au Stekerlapatte** (*r. des Prêtres 4; ✆ 512 8681; closed lunchtimes and Mon;* ●●), at the touristic but quaint **In't Spinnekopke** (*see page 30*) and at the eternally popular **La Grande Porte** (*see page 43*).

Belgium's chips (*frites*) are legendary. The French, the English and the Spanish all claim not only to have invented the chip but also to have the tastiest ones. But anyone who's ever eaten a portion of fries from a *friterie* (chip-stand) in Brussels knows that this accolade should rightfully go to the Belgians. So fanatical are they about their chips, there is even a website devoted to them (*www.belgianfries.com*), explaining how best to cook them, and why they are supreme.

The first known reference to the Belgian chip dates back to a manuscript dated 1781, entitled *Curiosités de la table dans le Pays-Bas Belges*, and informing the reader that 'the inhabitants of Belgium have the habit of frying small fish, which they catch in the Meuse, to improve their diet, specially the poor and needy. But when the frost comes and immobilizes the flow of the river, making fishing far too dangerous, the natives cut wedges of potatoes in the shape of little fish and fry them just like they would do with the fish. If I remember well this practice dates back over at least one hundred years...'.

The secret of Belgian *frites* is that they are cut quite thinly (but not as finely as French fries), fried twice (a process known as *double friture*) in beef-dripping, thus making them much crisper than their competitors. They are then tossed in the air to get rid of any excess oil. Brussels' chipmakers are also very particular about what sort of potato they use. Belgian potatoes are known for their flavour and variety, as the country's rich soil and cool climate creates ideal growing conditions. *Bintje*, or other floury, slightly sweet types are considered to make the best chips.

Belgian chips are *the* national snack, with *friterie* dotted throughout town serving huge portions of chips in paper cones called *frietzaks*. Every Bruxellois has their favourite one, but most will agree that **La Fritkot à Martin** (*on the corner of r. St-Josse and r. Verbist*) in Saint Josse, **La Friture St-Antoine** (*pl. Jourdan*) in Etterbeeck and **Homage à Mafrite** (*pl. du Jeu-de-Balle*) in Les Marolles are among the best. Most *friterie* open around 1000 and stay open until the early hours, seven days a week. Each

district has several to choose from: try **Friterie George** (*av. Du Parc, just off Barriere*) in Saint-Gilles, **La Grande Bouffe** (*pl. Fernand Cocq 17*) or **Chez George** (*r. de l'Acqueduct 4*) in Louise, **Friterie Persepolis** in place Sainte-Catherine, and **Fritland** (*r. Henri Maus 17*) near Grand-Place, with its choice of 12 different sauces.

The sauce smothered on top of your *frietzak* is the other essential aspect of eating chips in Brussels. No fries are complete without a sauce, and the Belgians have a legendary fondness for mayonnaise with theirs. Other dressings that you should try include tartare sauce, mustard, curry, ketchup, *harissa, americaine* (with a barbecue tang), pickle (similar to piccalilli), cocktail (with a touch of whisky!), *andalouse* (with tomatoes and herbs) and spicy pili-pili or chilli sauce … the choice is bewildering.

> **The natives cut wedges of potatoes in the shape of little fish and fry them just like they would do with fish.**

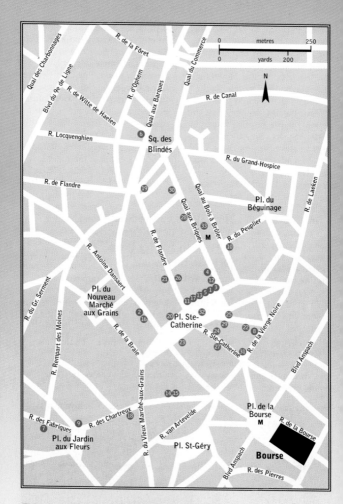

Place Sainte-Catherine

This smart district once formed the medieval heart of the city, and its main river port. Sadly, fishing boats no longer moor here as the river has long since been filled in, but fish shops and excellent seafood restaurants still line the ancient quaysides, while on rue Antoine Dansaert, trendy bars and bistros blend with the fashion boutiques.

PLACE SAINTE-CATHERINE
Restaurants

La Belle Maraichère ❶

Pl. Ste-Catherine 11

🕿 512 9759

Ⓜ Metro Sainte-Catherine

Open: Fri–Tue 1200–1415, 1800–2215

Reservations essential

All credit cards accepted

Seafood

€€€

Arguably the best fish restaurant in the Sainte-Catherine district, run by two brothers since 1973 with a loyal clientele of locals who appreciate the convivial atmosphere, excellent service, exceptional cuisine and good value for money. Ray and crab terrine, and grilled turbot with hop shoots count among the most popular dishes, together with such Flemish favourites as *waterzooi*, a stew made with three different types of fish.

Bonsoir Clara ❷

R. Antoine Dansaert 22

🕿 502 0990

Ⓜ Metro Bourse and Sainte-Catherine

Open: daily 1200–1430, 1900–2330 (Fri–Sat 2400)

Reservations essential

VISA 💳 American Express

European

€€€

One of the capital's trendiest restaurants, with two stunning dining rooms. The menu is essentially modern European, short and sweet, with French, Mediterranean and Belgian classics adapted to suit a savvy, cosmopolitan clientele. Typical dishes include sweetbreads with honey, or sea bream with pumpkin ravioli and coriander.

François ❸

Quai aux Briques 2

🕿 511 6089

Ⓜ Metro Sainte-Catherine

Open: Tue–Sun 1200–1430, 1830–2230

Reservations recommended

All credit cards accepted

Seafood

€€€

One of François's fortes is lobster. His special menu presents it in a variety of different ways: grilled, *au beurre de cérail* (tarragon and butter sauce), with Chinese spices, *à la nage* (with vegetables and cream sauce), thermidor … the list goes on. The kitchen opens on to the main dining room, where you can watch your meal

▲ Bonsoir Clara

being prepared. The second, more contemporary eating area leads into the adjoining fishy **delicatessen** (*pl. Ste-Catherine 12; open: Tue–Sat 0900–2200, Sun 0900–1900*).

L'Huîtrière  ❹

Quai aux Briques 20

∅ 512 0866

🚇 Metro Sainte-Catherine

Open: daily 1200–1500, 1900–2400

Reservations recommended

All credit cards accepted

Seafood

❸❸❸

As the name suggests, *hûitres* (oysters) are the speciality here (in season), but other highlights include turbot, sole, lobster and mussels, served by the kilo in a variety of different sauces.

In't Spinnekopke ❾

Pl. du Jardin aux Fleurs 1

∅ 511 8695

🚇 Metro Bourse

Open: Mon–Sat 1100–1500, 1800–2300 (Fri–Sat 2400), closed Sat lunch

Reservations essential

All credit cards accepted

Belgian

❷❷

Just five minutes' walk from the Stock Exchange, this celebrated *estaminet* (tavern) in a characterful little house dating from the 18th century is one of the capital's oldest restaurants and a veritable temple of authentic

Bruxelloise gastronomy. Above all, it is celebrated for its cuisine *à la bière* with such dishes as guinea fowl in raspberry beer, mussels with beer, even beer sorbets, as well as all the usual favourites.

Le Jardin de Catherine

Pl. Ste-Catherine 5–7

☎ 513 9262

Ⓜ Metro Sainte-Catherine

Open: daily 1200–1430, 1900–2300, closed Sat lunch

Reservations recommended

All credit cards accepted

Seafood-Belgian

€€€

This is truly a restaurant for all seasons, with a pavement terrace for spring and early autumn dining, an elegant but cosy dining room in winter and, in summer, a large and beautiful garden – a rarity in central Brussels and without doubt the highlight of this classy fish restaurant. The menu includes all the traditional favourites and a good choice of meat dishes to keep the carnivores happy too.

Le Loup-Galant

Quai aux Barques 4

☎ 219 9998

Ⓜ Metro Sainte-Catherine

Open: Tue–Sat 1200–1430, 1900–2200 (Fri–Sat 2230)

Reservations recommended

All credit cards accepted

French

€€€

Behind the elegant façade of this attractive 16th-century house near the fish market, Daniel Molmens, a chef of the great Flemish tradition, lovingly raises classic fish dishes to new heights with his inspired sauces. His *bouillabaisse* is celebrated throughout Brussels, as is his *gratinée* of mussels.

La Manufacture

R. Nôtre-Dame du Sommeil 12–22

☎ 502 2525

Ⓜ Metro Bourse and Port de Ninove

Open: Mon–Sat 1200–1400, 1900–2300 (Fri–Sat 2400), closed Sat lunch

Reservations essential

All credit cards accepted

Belgian

€€€

A smart restaurant housed in a most unlikely venue – inside a disused leather factory in a slightly run-down quarter of town. The building has been brilliantly converted, decked out in black and rust, with plenty of original piping, a metal staircase and a stylish terrace with cream parasols and bamboo. The food is modern Belgian with an Asian twist.

Au Thé de Pekin

R. de la Vierge Noire 16–24

☎ 513 4642

Ⓜ Metro Sainte-Catherine and De Brouckère

Open: daily 1200–1500, 1900–2300

Reservations recommended

All credit cards accepted

Chinese

€€

Another up-market restaurant, serving delicious Hong Kong cuisine, the speciality being *dim sum*, and a handful of other Far Eastern specialities at very reasonable prices. Some dishes have been added to the menu specifically to suit Belgian taste, including a variety of mussel dishes, and frogs legs in *hoi sin* sauce, while others – ducks' feet with oyster sauce, fish cheek hotpot and stuffed crabs claws – are truly authentic.

La Truit d'Argent ⑩

Quai aux Boix à Brûler 23

☎ 219 9546

Ⓜ Metro Sainte-Catherine

Open: Mon–Sat 1200–1430, 1900–2230, closed Sat lunch

Reservations recommended

All credit cards accepted

Seafood

€€€

The intimate, antique interior of 'The Silver Trout', with its cosy candlelit dining room and a terrace on the historic Marché aux Poissons, is the ideal venue for a special occasion. The predominantly seafood menu is renowned for its traditional quality and for the spectacular presentation of its dishes.

PLACE SAINTE-CATHERINE
Bars, cafés and pubs

L'Achepot ⑪

Pl. Ste-Catherine 1

✆ 511 6221

Ⓜ Metro Sainte-Catherine

Open: Mon–Sat 1100–1500, 1800–2400

Reservations recommended

No credit cards accepted

€

A popular, no-frills eatery, serving cheap, robust Bruxellois cuisine to locals and expats in simple surroundings. Offal dishes are the speciality, especially liver, kidneys, sweetbreads and brains. There's just a handful of small wooden tables inside and a pavement terrace overlooking the daily market in place Sainte-Catherine.

Les Crustacés ⑫

Quai aux Briques 8

✆ 513 1493

Ⓜ Metro Sainte-Catherine

Open: daily 1200–1500, 1800–2300

Reservations recommended

All credit cards accepted

€€

Of the many fish restaurants flanking the former river quaysides near place Sainte-Catherine, this 37-year-old family concern offers particularly good value with its set menus. Take a seat on the jolly yellow-and-white striped waterside terrace, don your special 'Les Crustacés' bib, arm yourself with a selection of pins, tongs and nutcrackers and tuck into the freshest of shellfish platters, garlic-grilled prawns, seafood casseroles and saucepans of steaming mussels.

L'Essentiel ⑬

Pl. Ste-Catherine 4

✆ 513 6834

Ⓜ Metro Sainte-Catherine

Open: daily 1200–1430, 1800–2300

Reservations recommended

All credit cards accepted

€€

This recently opened fish restaurant holds its own beside the age-old seafood institutions of Sainte-Catherine not only because of its insistence on the freshest of produce, but also for the originality of its cuisine – creative interpretations of old favourites, combining new flavours and textures.

Le Fin de Siècle ⑭

R. des Chartreux 9

✆ 513 5123

Ⓜ Metro Bourse

Open: Tue–Sun 1630–0100

VISA 💳

€€

An authentic Bruxellois late 19th-century café with its high ceiling, original bar, stained glass, a laid-back atmosphere, and satisfyingly filling food served until late at night. There's no menu, but rather an immense blackboard of choices, including soup of the day, spare ribs, rabbit in beer, chicken curry, and sausages with *stoemp*, washed down with a good choice of beers, *genevers* and wine by the glass.

Le Greenwich ⑮

R. des Chartreux 7

✆ 511 4167

Ⓜ Metro Bourse

Open: daily 1000–0100 (Fri–Sat 0200)

No credit cards accepted

€

At Le Greenwich, you're judged by just one standard: how well you play chess. That's why Réne Magritte didn't have much luck when he tried to sell his surrealist paintings to the café's patron a few decades ago. They figured that if he painted the way he played chess, his paintings were pretty worthless!

Kasbah ⑯

R. Antoine Dansaert 20

✆ 502 4026

⊙ Metro Bourse and Sainte-Catherine

Open: daily 1200–1400, 1900–2300 (Fri–Sat 2400)

Reservations essential at weekends

American Express

€€

This chic, vibrant Moroccan restaurant is a real Aladdin's cave with its dozens of multi-coloured lanterns which gleam like jewels, illuminating the midnight-blue interior. Choose from a large selection of *tagines*, couscous and other North African specialities.

I Latini

Pl. Ste-Catherine 2

✆ 502 5030

⊙ Metro Sainte-Catherine

Open: daily 1200–1430, 1800–2300 (Fri–Sat 2330)

All credit cards accepted

€€

The homemade pizzas, pasta and *calzone* here make a refreshing change from the abundant seafood restaurants in the area. Choose between a table in the 17th-century restaurant, decorated in commedia dell'arte style, or on the small pavement terrace overlooking the fruit and vegetable market.

Marina ⑱

R. des Chartreux 56

✆ 502 0636

⊙ Metro Bourse

Open: Mon–Sat 0730–2400

Reservations recommended

All credit cards accepted

€€

Marina's guiding principle is simplicity – of décor and of cuisine. The result: a charming, brilliant-red bistro adorned with culinary cartoon frescos from the 1930s, a tiny decked terrace at the back, and a small, market-fresh menu of pasta, meat and fish.

Strofilia

R. du Marché-aux-Porcs 13

✆ 512 3293

⊙ Metro Sainte-Catherine and Port de Flandre

Open: Mon–Sat 1900–2400

Reservations recommended at weekends

All credit cards accepted

€€

Don't expect any plate-smashing or traditional dancing here, as Strofilia is one of a spate of stylish, new-generation Greek restaurants opening in Brussels. It's hard to beat the setting – an atmospheric former wine depot, and a magical vaulted wine cellar, lit by candles. The restaurant serves over forty different *mezes* and counts the Prime Minister of Belgium and the Greek ambassador among its regulars.

La Villette ⑳

R. du Vieux Marché-aux-Grains

✆ 512 7550

⊙ Metro Sainte-Catherine

Open: Mon–Sat 1200–1430, 1830–2230, closed Sat lunch

All credit cards accepted

€

Hugely popular, especially in summer when the tables spill out on to the square, this country-style restaurant in the heart of the capital offers a large choice of wholesome Belgian fare. Try the *boudin* (black pudding) to start, served with chicory and onion relish, followed by salmon in a Hoegaerden (white beer) sauce, or steak *Breughel* (with cream, vegetables and *genever*).

▲ L'Achepot

PLACE SAINTE-CATHERINE
Shops, markets and picnic sites

Shops

De Boe 21

R. de Flandre

🅜 Metro Sainte-Catherine

Open: Tue–Sun 0900–1300, 1400–1800

No credit cards accepted

It's hard to resist this shop, with its delicious aroma of fresh coffee wafting into the street. With over a hundred years of coffee-roasting experience, De Boe offers all the traditional flavours and also some exceptional blends from all around the world, the most popular being 'Cérémonie'. The shop also sells connoisseur teas (the green tea with cardamom is divine), dried fruits, honey, chocolates, capers and wines.

Champigros 22

R. Melsens 22

🅜 Metro Sainte-Catherine and De Brouckère

Open: Tue–Sat 0730–1900

No credit cards accepted

This small street stall specialises in mushrooms of every shape, size and colour from tiny yellow shiitake, to bulbous brown *boletus* all imported from France, together with handsome garlic bulbs,

shallots, fresh herbs, white asparagus and truffles from Périgord.

Crèmerie de Linkebeek 23

R. Vieux Marché-aux-Grains 4

🅜 Metro Sainte-Catherine

Open: Mon–Sat 0800–1800

No credit cards accepted

A traditional 'dairy', decked out with huge metal milk churns, a black-and-white tiled floor covered in sawdust and serving ladies in old-fashioned aprons. The cheese counter is most impressive, with everything imaginable from runny brie to tiny *boutons de culotte* (trouser-button) goats' cheese. You can also buy milk, butter, eggs, olives, wines, quiches, honey and jam here, and toasted cheese sandwiches to eat on a park bench outside at lunchtime.

Espagne 24

R. Ste-Catherine

🅜 Metro Sainte-Catherine

Open: Tue–Sat 0800–1830, Sun 0800–1400

VISA

It's always a treat to enter this long-established cake shop and to marvel at its magnificent creations – the daintiest fruit tarts,

chocolate slices, crystallised fruits, waffles and *petit fours*. But the real *pièces de resistance* are the ice-cream gateaux in the display freezers. Children like the caterpillar- and the ladybird-shaped ones best and, for a loved one, how about a special present of an ice-cream 'bowl of roses'?

La Ferme Landaise 25

Pl. Ste-Catherine 41–3

🅜 Metro Sainte-Catherine

Open: Mon–Sat 0830–1800

All credit cards accepted

Most of the produce in this exclusive delicatessen comes from southwest France: conserves, *rillettes* (meat pastes), truffles, *cassoulets*, *foie gras*, smoked salmon, oils and vinegars, wines, champagnes and liqueurs. All very expensive.

Fraulein Schmitt 26

R. de Flandre 17

🅜 Metro Sainte-Catherine

Open: Tue–Fri 0900–1300, 1400–1800, Sat 0900–1700

No credit cards accepted

Not for vegetarians or the faint-hearted! One of the few remaining specialist tripe shops in Brussels, selling tongue, brain, stomach, liver, kidney and pretty much every other imaginable body part, together with tasty sausages, sauerkraut, pâtés and a variety of marinated meats ready for the barbecue.

Jean Guysels 27

R. Ste-Catherine 24

◉ Metro Sainte-Catherine

Open: Mon–Sat 0600–1830

No credit cards accepted

For generations this family butchers' has raised its own livestock and therefore knows exactly what it's selling to its customers – sausages, cold cuts, black puddings, salamis and tasty hormone-free joints of meat – reassuring in today's age of meat scandals.

La Maison du Caviar 28

Quai aux Briques 56

◉ Metro Sainte-Catherine

Open: Mon–Tue 0730–1200, Fri 0730–1600, Sat 0800–1200

All credit cards accepted

Specialist caviar dealers, selling six types of caviar, together with *foie gras*, smoked salmon and choice wines and champagnes.

Matthys & Van Gaever 29

R. Melsens

◉ Metro Sainte-Catherine and De Brouckère

Open: Tue–Sat 0700–1800

No credit cards accepted

Chicken, geese, turkeys, ducks, cuckoos, quails, pigeons ... you'll find them all here, hand-plucked, trussed ready for the pot, and displayed in rows in this specialist poultry shop.

Nielsvins 30

Quai aux Briques 76–8

◉ Metro Sainte-Catherine

Open: Tue–Sun 1000–1900

A smart, modernist shop at the heart of the Vismet fish market zone, specialising in predominantly French wines and, needless to say, with a good choice of bottles to accompany fish dishes.

Sunwah 31

R. de la Vierge Noire

◉ Metro Bourse

Open: Mon–Sat 0900–1900

No credit cards accepted

A huge Chinese supermarket packed full with Asian shoppers from the large local community living here.

Markets

Marché aux Fruits et Légumes 32

Pl. Ste-Catherine

◉ Metro Sainte-Catherine

Open: daily 0700–1700

No credit cards accepted

This photogenic clutter of colourful stalls sells fresh market-garden produce, plants and flowers on a daily basis, with the curvaceous baroque belfry of the church of Sainte-Catherine as a backdrop.

Vismet – Vieux Marché aux Poissons 33

Quai aux Briques and Quai aux Bois à Brûler

◉ Metro Sainte-Catherine

Open: daily 0400–1300

No credit cards accepted

The old fish market, known locally as Vismet, takes place every morning along the ancient quays here, and early risers will find it interesting to see the lorries unloading the day's catch at dawn.

▲ Place Sainte-Catherine

Mussels – the national dish

Famed across the world

There is no denying it, Brussels is a seafood lover's paradise. Belgians are known to be among the biggest fish and shellfish eaters in Europe. No matter where you are in Belgium, the sea is never far away and, as a result, they have developed an extensive seafood cuisine. From juicy eels in a luxurious fresh herb sauce (*anguilles au vert*), and fresh herring baked in individual paper packets (*harengs en papillote*) to *moules-frites* – tender, steamed mussels accompanied by a bowl of freshly made Belgian chips with lashings of creamy mayonnaise.

Moules-frites are a way of life in Brussels. Everywhere you go you'll find them on the menu, a classic and delicious combination which comes as close as anything to being Belgium's national dish. The mussels all originate from the cold North Sea waters off Zeeland. Like oysters, mussels are a seasonal food. They reach their peak during cooler months and, according to an old fisherman's saying, they should be eaten only during months that contain the letter 'r' (September to April). During these months, there are nightly deliveries to place Sainte-Catherine, home to Brussels' best seafood restaurants. Some of the tourist restaurants off the Grand-Place and in rue des Bouchers cook mussels all year round, but be warned – many of their mussels are frozen and no self-respecting Bruxellois would contemplate eating them out of season!

It is said that mussels are good for you – low in fat and cholesterol, packed full of protein, vitamins and minerals and 'full of the strength of the sea'. They are inexpensive and easy to cook. The main criteria are that they must be alive when you buy them and they must remain alive until you cook them. They need to be at their peak of freshness for a favourite Brussels starter – eaten raw like oysters, straight from their shells with a squeeze of lemon.

Most mussel fans eat them as a main course served by the kilo in their shells, with a mound of crispy golden fries. There is a closely observed etiquette for eating them correctly. The whole pot is brought, piping-hot, to the table, along with a big empty bowl for the shells. You may use a

▲ Mussel pots

fork to eat your first mussel, but for the rest you're supposed to use that first mussel shell as a pincer to pick out the remaining mussels from their shells. It is perfectly acceptable practice to eat the accompanying chips with your fingers (after all, they taste better that way!) or again by using the mussel shell. At the end of the meal, it is normal to have a few slurps of the cooking juices. A spoon is always provided.

There are countless different ways in which to cook a pot full of *moules*. Traditionally, they are steamed with aromatic herbs, leeks, celery and onions (*marinière*); cooked with white wine and cream (*au vin blanc*) or in tomatoes and garlic (*provençale*). However, in recent years new recipes have emerged, with some restaurants boasting such exotic dishes as *moules à l'hydromel* (with honey and crème fraiche), *moules à l'escargot* (with snail butter), *moules à l'écossaise* (with whisky), even *moules au champagne*. Specialist restaurant **La Moulière** (*pl. Ste-Catherine 23; Ø 219 6549; closed Apr–Aug; reservations recommended;* ❷❷) features mussels cooked 34 different ways, including 'Extra Mussels' – *moules* cooked in lobster bisque, fresh shrimps and cognac.

Other top *moules* restaurants in the Sainte-Catherine area include **La Belle Maraichère** (*see page 29*), **François** (*see page 29*)

▲ Mussels

and **Le Pre Salé** (*r. de Flandre 20; Ø 513 4323; closed Mon; reservations recommended;* ❷❷). In the trendy Saint-Boniface district near Louise, **Au Vieux Bruxelles** (*r. St-Boniface 35; closed May–Aug;* ❷❷) serves mussels in a variety of different sauces, including curry, and spicy paprika sauce, in a cosy bistro setting with jolly red-and-white checked tablecloths and pitchers of robust house wine. **Léon** (*see page 12*) is perhaps the most famous (and inevitably the most touristic) venue for mussels in town. **Au Boeuf Gros Sel** (*r. Jourdan 8; Ø 538 1195; closed Sun;* ❷❷) serves its wide choice of mussel dishes on a sunny terrace in Saint-Gilles (try them in snail butter or green pepper sauce). **Scheltema** (*r. des Dominicains 7; Ø 512 2084; closed Sun; reservations recommended;* ❷❷) is one of few seafood restaurants off Grand-Place worth trying: an elegant brasserie unafraid of simplicity, where mussels are cooked *marinière, au vin blanc* and *provençale*. The choice is yours.

> It is said that mussels are good for you – low in fat and cholesterol, packed full of protein, vitamins and minerals and 'full of the strength of the sea'.

Le Sablon

The aristocratic Le Sablon district is known for its gastronomic restaurants, its antique shops and its chic pavement cafés and bars – the place to see and be seen in Brussels. By contrast, the run-down, working-class neighbourhood of Les Marolles contains a mass of more down-to-earth eateries, some lively bars and the city's main flea market, although of late this district too has begun to acquire a new, chic charm.

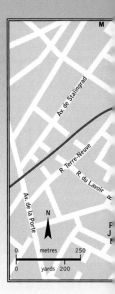

LE SABLON
Restaurants

Chez Marius en Provence ❶

Pl. du Petit Sablon 1

✆ 511 1208

🚊 Trams 92, 93 and 94

Open: Mon–Sat 1200–1430, 1900–2230

Reservations recommended

All credit cards accepted

French

€€€

Chef Marius seduces the beautiful people of Le Sablon at this 17th-century restaurant with his repertoire of Mediterranean dishes, including courgette flowers stuffed with lobster, artichoke soufflé, sea wolf cooked in a salt crust and his legendary *bouillabaisse*.

L'Écailler du Palais Royal ❷

R. Bodenbroek 18

✆ 512 8751

🚌 Buses 20, 34, 48, 95 and 96 or trams 92, 93 and 94

Open: Mon–Sat 1200–1430, 1900–2300, closed Aug

Reservations essential

All credit cards accepted

Seafood

€€€

A sublime seafood restaurant at the heart of Le Sablon, sophisticated yet welcoming, with impeccable service, refined cuisine and an outstanding wine list. The menu is traditional, changing with the seasons, and includes such delicacies as lobster ravioli, and sea devil with linden butter.

L'Estrille du Vieux Bruxelles ❸

R. de Rollebeek 7

✆ 512 5857

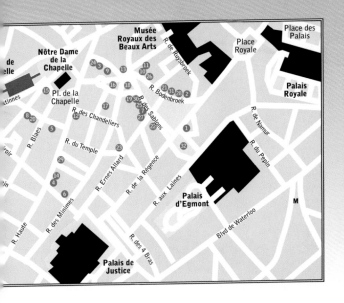

⊙ Buses 20, 34, 48, 95 and 96

Open: daily 1200–2400

Reservations recommended

All credit cards accepted

Belgian

€€

Constructed in 1587, L'Estrille was originally a coaching inn, built on the ancient ramparts of the city. Specialities include homemade ducks' liver terrine, and mussels, followed by a genuine *café liégois* – coffee ice cream, *genever* and whipped cream. In summer special gastronomic menus are served in the courtyard during the *Nocturnes du Sablon* classical music festival,

and in December there's even a live donkey here.

Le Gourmandine ④

R. Haute 125

✆ 512 9892

⊙ Buses 20 and 48

Open: daily 1200–1430, 1900–2200, closed Sat lunch, Sun evening and Mon evening

Reservations recommended

All credit cards accepted

French

€€–€€€

Jean-Bernard van Hauw's imaginative creations include langoustines perfumed with honey and mint, *poulard de Bresse* with garlic, tapenade and pears, and fish tart with

an asparagus compote. The market menu and the gourmand menu merit special attention, as does the bitter chocolate mousse filled with orange crème brûlée.

L'Idiot du Village ⑤

R. Nôtre-Seigneur 19

✆ 502 5582

⊙ Buses 20 and 48

Open: Mon–Fri 1200–1400, 1930–2300

Reservations essential

All credit cards accepted

French

€€€

Hidden down a side street off rue Blaes, there's something very endearing about this tiny bistro with its two

dishes as lobster with vanilla and *cabillaud au cerfeuil*), his performance deserves heartfelt applause.

Lola ⑦

Pl. du Grand Sablon 33

∅ 514 2460

🚌 Buses 20, 34, 48, 95 and 96 or trams 92, 93 and 94

Open: daily 1200–1500, 1830–2330

Reservations recommended

💳 💳 American Express

French

💰💰

The menu here is classically French but with a twist – duck with mango and rabbit with almonds and orange blossom count among the main courses – and there are plenty of salads and vegetarian dishes. Lola's clientele is predominantly smart, young and executive.

Les Petits Oignons ⑧

R. Nôtre-Seigneur 13

∅ 512 4738

🚌 Buses 20 and 48

Open: Mon–Sat 1200–1430, 1900–2300, closed Aug

💳 ⓓ American Express

French

💰💰

Ask for a table in the flower-bedecked garden and order goats' cheese grilled with thyme, chicory and a tomato coulis, followed by salmon roasted with lemon and lavender-scented honey, accompanied by good wines at

pint-sized dark dining rooms, its motley assortment of wall paintings, its exuberant chandeliers and kitsch baroque-style furniture, yet it remains an eternal favourite among city-dwellers, who come for its unique romantic-comic atmosphere and its exceptional market-fresh cuisine.

Le Joueur de Flûte ⑥

R. de l'Épée 26

∅ 513 4311

🚌 Buses 20 and 48 or trams 92, 93 and 94

Open: Mon–Fri 2000–2130

Reservations essential

💳 💳

French

💰💰💰

Chef Philippe van Cappelen orchestrates exquisite dishes with great virtuosity, carefully selecting a different menu each night. Having tasted the culinary delights (which typically include such reasonable prices. There's even a complimentary car-parking service at lunchtimes.

La Tortue du Zoute 9

R. de Rollebeek 31

✆ 513 1062

🚍 Buses 20, 34, 48, 95 or 96

Open: 1900–2330, closed Sun evening and Tue

Reservations recommended

All credit cards accepted

Seafood

€€€

It's *de rigueur* to order lobster here, cooked in a variety of ways: with butter and Sauternes, grilled with fresh herbs, *à la nage, en civet aux legumes de saison* or *façon La Tortue*.

La Tour d'y Voir 10

Pl. du Grand Sablon 8–9

✆ 511 4043

🚍 Buses 20, 34, 48, 95 and 96 or trams 92, 93 and 94

Open: Tue–Sun 1200–1430, 1930–2300

Reservations recommended

All credit cards accepted

French

€€

It's hard to find a more romantic setting for a special occasion than La Tour d'y Voir, housed in a converted 14th-century chapel, with atmospheric brick-clad interior, intimate candlelit tables and stained-glass windows. The contemporary French cuisine is of the highest quality, and the special 'surprise' and 'prestige' menus are especially good value.

Trente Rue de la Paille 11

R. de la Paille 30

✆ 512 0715

🚍 Buses 20, 34, 48, 95 and 96 or trams 92, 93 and 94

Open: Mon–Fri 1200–1430, 1900–2330

Reservations recommended

💳 American Express

French

€€€

Hidden round the corner from place du Grand Sablon in a small, old mansion, this cosy, elegant restaurant with rustic wooden beams and exposed brickwork, is famous for the highly original culinary creations of André Martiny, chef here for the past twenty years. Specialities frequently combine two complementary meats or fish in one dish, such as roast pigeon and smoked quail in truffle juice, or roast langoustine tails served with pan-fried strips of duck liver and almonds.

LE SABLON
Bars, cafés and pubs

L'Arrosoir ⑫

R. Haute 60

☎ 502 0068

🚌 Buses 20 and 48

Open: Tue–Sun 1200–1430, 1900–2300 (Fri–Sat 2330), closed Sun evening

💳

€

Decked out like a green-house, with wooden cane fencing for walls, buckets of flowers and a glass-paned roof hung with metal *arrosoirs* (watering-cans), this newly opened bistro serves an unremarkable menu of international cuisine (spare ribs, Thai curry, steaks, salads), but its generous portions are guaranteed to satiate the hungriest of gardeners.

Aux Bons Enfants ⑬

Pl. du Grand Sablon 49

☎ 512 4095

🚌 Buses 20, 34, 48, 95 and 96

Open: Thu–Tue 1200–1445, 1830–2230

No credit cards accepted

€

A lively Le Sablon favourite – dark, smoky and authentically Bruxellois, with its basic décor, wooden tables, paper tablecloths and simple but hearty menu of soups, pasta, fish and steak dishes.

Boulangerie de la Chapelle ⑭

R. Haute 146

☎ 511 5619

🚌 Buses 20 and 48

Open: Tue–Fri 0730–1930, Sun 0730–1530

No credit cards accepted

€

This striking bakery-cum-café decorated with original art-nouveau tiles serves up quiches, pastries,

all-day breakfasts, a couple of *plats du jour* and an excellent buffet brunch on Sundays (*1000–1500*) in its peaceful back room.

Les Brigittines 'Aux Marchés de la Chapelle' ⑮

Pl. de la Chapelle 5

☎ 512 6891

🚌 Buses 20 and 48

Open: Mon–Thu 1200–1400, 1900–2300, Fri 1200–1430, 1900–2400, Sat 1900–2400, closed Sat lunch and Aug

All credit cards accepted

€€

Alongside the Church of Nôtre-Dame de la Chapelle, this authentic Bruxellois brasserie serves such staples as prawn croquettes, Zebrugge sole poached with leeks and roast lamb with tarragon in an atmospheric belle-époque setting.

La Canne à Sucre ⑯

R. des Pigeons 12

☎ 513 0372

🚌 Buses 20, 34, 48, 95 and 96

Open: Tue–Sat 1930–0030 (Fri–Sat 0130)

No credit cards accepted

€€

For a wild night out, this tiny, eccentric Caribbean restaurant-

▲ Au Chat Perché

bar serves up spicy Antilles cuisine (Caribbean fish soup, Creole crab claws) with over 250 rum-based cocktails, and live music on Thursday, Friday and Saturday.

Au Chat Perché

R. de la Samaritaine 20

✆ 513 5213

🚍 Buses 20, 34, 48, 95 and 96 to Grand Sablon

Open: Tue–Sun 1200–1400, 1900–2230, closed Sat lunch and Sun lunch

No credit cards accepted

€€

Hidden down a backstreet in Les Marolles district near the famous weekend flea market at place du Jeu-de-Balle, this small, cosy bistro has an imaginative menu combining French, Asian and Mediterranean cuisine in such dishes as filet of sea bream with honey, ginger and lime, duck with port and orange, and scampi in a light curry sauce.

Chez Richard

R. des Minimes 2

✆ 512 1406

🚍 Buses 20, 34, 48, 95 and 96

Open: Mon–Sat 0700–0200, Sun 0900–0100

No credit cards accepted

€

At lunchtimes the basic *plats du jour* (tripe, grilled chicken) attract local businessmen to this rough and ready, typically Marollien bar. In the afternoon locals

while away the time reading the papers and playing cards; by night a younger set crowd the bar to enjoy its cellar-cool Kriek beer.

L'Entrée des Artistes

Pl. du Grand Sablon 42

✆ 502 3161

🚍 Buses 20, 34, 48, 95 and 96 or trams 92, 93 and 94

Open: daily 1200–2400

🚏 American Express

€

One of the more affordable bars lining Le Sablon, where you can linger awhile over a drink on the pavement terrace, or tuck into steak, quiche or salad from the list of daily specials chalked up on the blackboard menu.

La Grande Porte

R. Nôtre-Seigneur 9

✆ 512 8998

🚍 Buses 20 and 48 to Chapelle

Open: Mon–Sat 1200–1500, 1800–0200, closed Sat lunch

🚏

€€

Tuck into mighty portions of *waterzooi*, *carbonnade à la Flamande*, and chicken cooked in Kriek and cherries at this convivial, family-run restaurant, decorated with Belgian cartoons and hidden down a back alley in Les Marolles.

La Kartchma

Pl. du Grand Sablon 17

✆ 512 4310

🚍 Buses 20, 34, 48, 95 and 96 or trams 92, 93 and 94

Open: daily 0900–0100

🚏

€

Park up your cabriolet, don your shades, order your *antipasti*, and get ready to see and be seen at the outside tables of this trendy Le Sablon bar, wedged between two other equally popular bars (**Le Malcour** and **Le Grain de Sable**) and overlooking the weekend antiques market.

Le Pain Quotidien

R. des Sablons 11

✆ 513 5154

🚍 Trams 92, 93 and 94

Open: Mon–Fri 0730–1900, Wed and Sat–Sun 0800–1900

All credit cards accepted

€

The most impressive of a growing chain of bakery-cafés, each with a country-kitchen feel, with large pine tables and wooden dressers packed with jams, condiments, ciders and coffees to buy. Their open sandwiches, quiches, salads and patisseries make an ideal lunch snack, best enjoyed in the shady garden out at the back.

▲ La Kartchma

Le Perroquet ㉓

R. Watteeu 31

✆ 512 9922

🚋 Trams 92, 93 and 94

Open: daily 1000–0100

No credit cards accepted

€

Join the in-crowd of Le Sablon at this genuine art-nouveau bar, with its original mirrors, stained glass, marble-topped tables and black-and-white tiled floor, and snack on speciality stuffed pitta breads.

Be sure to save room for the delicious gateaux for afters! A takeaway service is also available.

The Tea House ㉔

R. de Rollebeek 5

✆ 511 8117

🚌 Buses 20, 34, 48, 95 and 96

Open: daily 1100–1900

No credit cards accepted

€

For that special cuppa, the tranquil upstairs *salon de thé* here offers a wide variety of teas

from around the world, accompanied by calorific chocolate cakes and fruit tarts. The shop below sells teapots, tea towels, tea strainers … even teabags for the bath.

Au Vieux St-Martin ㉕

Pl. du Grand Sablon 38

✆ 512 6476

🚌 Buses 20, 34, 48, 95 and 96 or trams 92, 93 and 94

Open: daily 1000–2400

All credit cards accepted

€

This modern brasserie with a distinct café atmosphere and pavement terrace is eternally popular, thanks to its classic Belgian menu including *waterzooi*, Ardennes sausage, *stoemp* and other old favourites.

Wittamer ㉖

Pl. du Grand Sablon 12–13

✆ 512 3742

🚌 Buses 20, 34, 48, 95 and 96 to Grand Sablon or trams 92, 93 and 94 to Petit Sablon

Open: Mon 0900–1800, Tue–Sat 0700–1900, Sun 0700–1800

All credit cards accepted

€

Wittamer's teashop attracts an exclusive clientele, prepared to pay over the odds for its highly reputed name. Each patisserie is a veritable work of art, almost too good to eat. The Wittamer chocolate shop is a couple of doors away at no 6.

LE SABLON
Shops, markets and picnic sites

Shops

Claire Fontaine 27

R. Ernes Allard 3

🚌 Buses 20, 34, 48, 95 and 96 or trams 92, 93 and 94

Open: daily 1000–1900 (Sat 1800)

No credit cards accepted

Just off place du Grand Sablon, this pint-sized traditional delicatessen is packed from floor to ceiling with pâtés, terrines, cheeses, smoked salmon, cold cuts, olives and artichokes.

The Linen House 28

R. Bodenbroek 10

🚃 Trams 92, 93 and 94

Open: Mon–Sat 0900–1830

💳 💳

Chic Le Sablon shoppers come to this small, unlikely looking shop to buy their exclusive table linen. Folded neatly in orderly drawers and shelves is a dazzling selection of quality cotton and linen tablecloths, napkins and matching oven gloves.

New de Wolf 29

R. Blaes 40

🚌 Buses 20 and 48

Open: Mon–Tue and Thu–Sat 1000–1830, Sun 1000–1500

All credit cards accepted

An enormous shop, stretching from rue Blaes to rue Haute, full of stylish yet affordable household goods, ranging from elegant glassware and porcelain dinner services to trendy napkin rings, pepper grinders and barbecue equipment.

Pierre Marcolini 30

Pl. du Grand Sablon 39

🚌 Buses 20, 34, 48, 95 and 96 or trams 92, 93 and 94

Open: Mon–Sat 1000–1900

All credit cards accepted

This young, prize-winning chocolate-maker is world-renowned in confectionery circles for his remarkable chocolate and sugar sculptures. Even if you don't intend to buy, do help yourself to a spoonful of warm melted chocolate pouring from the fountain at the back of the shop!

La Vaisselle au Kilo 31

R. Bodenbroek 8a

🚃 Trams 92, 93 and 94

Open: Mon–Sat 1000–1800, Sun 1000–1730

💳 💳

An Aladdin's cave of crockery and glassware. The name means 'dishes by the kilo' and that's exactly how you buy it (although some items can be bought individually).

Picnic sites

Place du Petit Sablon 32

Southeast of r. de la Regence

🚃 Trams 92, 93 and 94

This charming square, opposite Brussels' finest Gothic church, the church of Nôtre-Dame de la Chapelle, is enclosed by art-nouveau railings and a series of columns, each surmounted by a statuette representing one of the medieval guilds of Brussels.

▲ Claire Fontaine

Chocolate – a magic word!

"'Chocolate' – a magic word! Say it loud, and faces light up ... Is there anyone who does not have a warm and tasty chocolate memory somewhere in his life?" (Jean Galler, chocolate-maker to the King of Belgium)

Belgian chocolate is the finest in the world, and the nation's greatest pride. The Belgians themselves are passionate choco-holics, consuming an average 7.4kg a head per year. Daily life without chocolate in Brussels would be unimaginable. There's a chocolate shop in pretty much every street, luring passers-by in with their dazzling window displays and the tantalising, sweet smell of melted chocolate. Many people start their day by smearing thick chocolate spread on to a slice of bread for breakfast. Hot chocolate is served in many cafés and is especially popular in winter. Children enjoy chocolate milk, puddings lean heavily on chocolate, there's even a chocolate-flavoured beer, and nobody appears empty-handed at the door of friends or relatives without the ubiquitous box of chocolates.

Why is Belgian chocolate better than any other? Because it uses the world's best ingredients – cocoa beans from Africa (which are stronger and more assertive than the milder South American beans favoured by other nations' *chocolatiers*) with a minimum of 70 per cent cocoa solids, fresh cream, cocoa butter (rather than vegetable fat used in inferior-quality chocolate) and no preserving agents. The result: the world's best chocolates – quality, sumptuous confections, but with a limited shelf life. To find out more about the manufacture and history of Belgian chocolate, there's a **Chocolate Museum** in the centre of town (*Grand-Place 13; Ø 514 2048; open: Tue–Sun 1000– 1700*). Alternatively, visit Frank Duval, dubbed the 'Willy-Wonka of Brussels' at **Planète Chocolat** where he demonstrates the 'art of chocolate' on Saturday afternoons (*see page 15*).

▲ Neuhaus chocolates

The most famous Belgian chocolate manufacturers are **Leonidas, Godiva** and **Neuhaus**, with branches all over the country and abroad. Leonidas is the most affordable of the big names. They turn over a staggering 6 000 tonnes of chocolate each year and their unique shops, with counters opening on to the pavement, offer customers a kind of 'fast-food' chocolate service.

Jean Neuhaus first founded a 'pharmaceutical confectioners' at Galerie de la Reine 25-7 (*see page 15*), producing cough sweets, bars of bitter chocolate and liquorice for stomach complaints. With a growing market for sweet confectionery, the old pharmacy soon became the first and finest *chocolaterie* in the city. **Neuhaus** also invented the first filled chocolate, giving it the name 'praline'. Today *pralinen* are the highest achievement of the chocolate-maker's art – a beautifully sculpted chocolate shell in a variety of shapes filled with any number of delicious fillings. Neuhaus then invented the *ballotin* (chocolate box), as a result of increasing dissatisfaction with the bags used in the store at that time, as they caused the pralines to be unnecessarily squashed and damaged.

Godiva (*Grand-Place 21, blvd Adolphe Max 89 and Chaussée de Charleroi 43*) enjoys the greatest international reputation, with over 1 400 shops worldwide,

▲ Godiva chocolates

selling 120 different kinds of luxury praline, including *gianduja* (chocolate cream and crushed almonds), *ganache* (chocolate, cream and butter), *manon* (pure fresh cream), liqueurs and any number of mousse and fruit cream fillings. The shop was named after Lady Godiva, the 11th-century nobleman's wife who rode naked through the streets of Coventry. In 1929 the founders thought the image represented the qualities of their chocolates – rich, elegant, daring and sensual.

But don't just visit the big names in chocolate manufacture, or you will be missing out on the very finest of Belgian chocolate. Some of the capital's top confectioners are individual concerns with just one or two outlets, producing the most sensational, handcrafted *pralinen*. No chocolate fan should come to Brussels without visiting the legendary stores of **Wittamer** (*Place du Grand Sablon 9*), **Mary** (*r. Royale 73*), **Galler,** royal warrant holders (*see page 25*), and prize-winning **Pierre Marcolini** (*see page 45*), whose divine chocolate sculptures represent the pinnacle of Belgian chocolate mastery.

> **The Belgians are passionate chocoholics, consuming an average 7.4kg a head per year.**

EU District

Although largely an area of traffic-choked boulevards and uncompromising office blocks forming the administrative centre of Europe, all those Eurocrats and their staff do need to eat and drink (many of them on vast expense accounts)! As a result, the EU district contains more than its fair share of gourmet restaurants, as well as a surprising number of snack-bars, pubs and bistros.

EU DISTRICT
Restaurants

Atelier Européen ❶

R. Franklin 28

Ø 734 9140

Ⓜ Metro Schuman

Open: Mon–Fri 1200–1430, 1900–2200, closed Aug

Reservations essential at lunchtimes

All credit cards accepted

French

❸❸❸

More a restaurant for gourmands than gourmets, L'Atelier is frequented by a lively set of Eurocrats from the nearby Berlaimont

Centre who enjoy the sensational eat-as-much-as-you-want lunchtime buffet, accompanied by the highly palatable house wine (charged per centimetre). Customers are served in a small, leafy courtyard or inside the airy restaurant. Evenings are more tranquil with an à la carte menu offering such delicacies as grilled sole with prawns and saffron, and sweet and sour duck braised in red fruits.

Chez Callens ❷

Hôtel Marie-José, r. du Commerce 73

Ø 512 0843

Ⓜ Metro Trône

Open: Mon–Fri 1200–1500, 1800–2200

Reservations recommended at lunchtimes

All credit cards accepted

French-Belgian

❸❸❸

Businessmen and politicians alike frequent this restaurant's small, conservative dining rooms for the 'Quick Lunch'

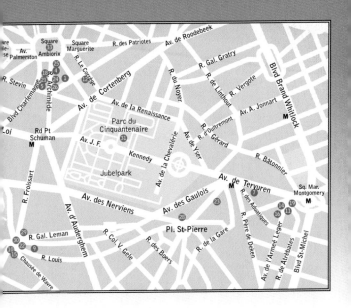

and 'Business Lunch' set menus, and also for its sophisticated evening à la carte. The weekly changing menu, based on fresh market produce, includes such old-fashioned favourites as shrimp croquettes and *waterzooi à la gantoise* (chicken in a vegetable, lemon and cream sauce), together with more innovative dishes such as carpaccio of aubergine and rocket, and turbot in caper sauce. The hotel cellar contains a staggering 20,000-plus bottles.

Les Continents ③

Hôtel Europa Inter-Continental, r. de la Loi 107

✆ 230 1333
Ⓜ Metro Maelbeek
Open: daily 0700–1030, 1200–1430, 1900–2230
Reservations recommended
All credit cards accepted
French-Mediterranean
❸❸❸

This refined restaurant serves an eclectic choice of imaginative French and Mediterranean dishes and, according to the restaurant motto, it

is 'a cuisine full of sunshine, flavour and simplicity'. Tuck into crab and citrus fruit gazpacho or pan-fried duck liver with potato cake, prunes and papaya in cider vinegar.

Le Jardin d'Espagne ④

R. Archimède 65
✆ 736 3449
Ⓜ Metro Schuman or bus 22
Open: Mon–Fri 1200–1500, 1900–2200, Sat 1900–2200
Reservations unnecessary
All credit cards accepted
Spanish
❸❸

The cooking here is simple and honest and

without frills. The menu boasts all the usual Spanish staples, such as serrano ham, delicious mixed fish grills and *crema catalana*. For a lighter snack, try the **Bodeguilla**, a *tapas* bar hidden in the basement (*open: 1200–0200*), which serves small portions of spicy *chorizo* sausage, anchovies, squid, mushrooms, octopus and meatballs, all washed down with jugs of homemade sangria.

Au Plaisir ⑤

Hôtel Dorint, blvd Charlemagne 11–19

Ø 231 0909

🅜 Metro Schuman

Open: Mon–Fri 1200–1500, 1830–2230

Reservations recommended

All credit cards accepted

French

€€€

In this artily designed restaurant, the equally 'designer' menu includes lobster with sour cream and parsley juice, scampi steamed with seaweed and served with a cooked apple parcel in a light curry sauce. For an unusual but trendy dessert, try a slice of potato with warm Munster cheese and salad.

Salon des Anges

Hôtel Léopold Brussels, r. du
Luxembourg 35

✆ 511 1828

Ⓜ Metro Trône

Open: Mon–Sat 1200–1500,
1900–2200, closed Sat
lunch

Reservations recommended

All credit cards accepted

Belgian

●●●

Flemish head chef Peter
Maertens enjoys a
seasonal repertoire, with
monthly changing
menus including hop
shoots in April,
asparagus in May and
truffles in October. À la
carte specialities include
lobster ravioli, roast
cuckoo with turnips and
savoy cabbage and a
variety of flambée
dishes, and there is an
impressive wine list to
match.

Le Serpolet ❼

Av. de Tervuren 59

✆ 736 1701

Ⓜ Metro Merode or trams
81 and 82

Open: daily 1200–1430,
1900–2200, closed Sat
lunch and Sun evening

Reservations recommended

All credit cards accepted

French

●●●

Everything at Le
Serpolet is *comme il
faut*. With over fifteen
years at the reins,
patron-chef Claude
Vanderhulst has firmly
established his reputa-
tion as a gourmet chef
of the highest calibre.

His charming restaurant
offers such gastronomic
delights as Provençal
roast lamb with thyme
flowers, and red mullet
in a pastry case with
goats' cheese, grilled
aubergines and tomato
conserve.

Stanhope-Brighton ❽

Hôtel Stanhope, r. du
Commerce 9

✆ 506 9555

Ⓜ Metro Trône

Open: Mon–Fri 1200–1430,
1900–2200

Reservations recommended

All credit cards accepted

French

●●●

Hôtel Stanhope was the
first five-star hotel to
be appointed in
Brussels, and its gastro-
nomic restaurant, 'The
Brighton', offers some
of the finest French
cuisine in town. Its
oriental décor is
inspired by the Royal
Pavilion at Brighton,
and there is even a
leafy interior garden for
summer al fresco
dining. The restaurant
serves a mainly execu-
tive clientele, and there
is an excellent four-
course business menu at
midday.

Stirwen ❾

Chaussée St-Pierre 15–17

✆ 640 8541

Ⓜ Buses 34, 59 and 80

Open: Mon–Fri 1200–1400,
1900–2130

Reservations recommended

All credit cards accepted

French

●●

A popular bistro with
cosy art-nouveau-
inspired décor, serving
good value-for-money
comfort food from the
provinces of France. Be
sure to try the
Burgundian beef or a
hearty *cassoulet*!

Vimar ❿

Pl. Jourdan 70

✆ 213 0949

Ⓜ Buses 34, 59 and 80

Open: Mon–Sat 1200–1430,
1900–2145, closed Sat
lunch

Reservations recommended

〓 American Express

Seafood

●●

One of a cluster of
eateries in up-and-com-
ing place Jourdan, this
small, smart restaurant
specialises in the fresh-
est of fish, with a daily
changing menu depend-
ing on the catch of the
day. Specialities include
sashimi with three mus-
tards for starters, and
bouillabaisse or a mixed
shellfish platter to fol-
low, accompanied by
crisp French white
wines.

LE
PAIN

QUOTIDIEN
du Quartier Léopold

EU DISTRICT
Bars, cafés and pubs

Anis et Vanille 11

Av. de l'Armée 2

✆ 735 0786

🚇 Metro Montgomery or trams 81 and 82

Open: Mon–Fri 1200–1430, 1900–2230, Sat 1900–2230

All credit cards accepted

💶💶

This modern restaurant's menu is ingeniously divided into four food genres to suit all tastes – Japanese, Thai, Chinese and Vietnamese, each offering soups, starters, main courses and desserts. Either mix and match or simply stick to one nationality. The Japanese *tempura*, the Thai spicy soups and the Vietnamese five-spiced beef *brochettes* with lemongrass are highly recommended.

L'Atlantide 12

R. Franklin 73

✆ 736 2002

🚇 Metro Schuman or buses 21 and 82

Open: Mon–Sat 1200–1430, 1900–2300

💳💶

💶

Hidden up a back-street, this small, traditional, blue-and-white taverna is especially popular with Greek expats working in the EU district, who enjoy the fresh grilled fish, the simple *plat du jour*, and the sticky *baklava*, washed down with copious quantities of *retsina*.

Chez Moi 13

R. du Luxembourg 66

✆ 280 2666

🚇 Metro Trône

Open: Mon–Fri 1200–1500, 1900–2200

Reservations essential at lunchtimes

All credit cards accepted

💶💶

Ideally located near the European Parliament building, this small, minimalist restaurant, with an open kitchen and pavement terrace, focuses all its attention on its simple, daily changing French-Belgian menu which features such market-fresh delights as asparagus, chicken in chicory sauce, grilled sardines and at least one vegetarian dish.

La Duchesse 14

Av. de Tervuren 134

✆ 732 4331

🚇 Metro Montgomery or trams 81 and 82

Open: Mon–Fri 1200–1430, 1800–2300, Sat 1700–2300

All credit cards accepted

💶💶

The sunny terrace of this popular brasserie is always packed at lunchtime and early evening, with locals tucking into the wholesome menu of *stoemp* with sausages, coq au vin, *pierrades* (a choice of raw meats to cook yourself on a hot stone slab at your table) and mussels in season.

L'Esprit du Sel 15

Pl. Jourdan 52

✆ 230 6040

🚇 Buses 34, 59 and 80

Open: daily 1200–2400

Reservations recommended

💳 American Express

💶💶

This small bistro carefully juxtaposes rustic bare brick and pine tables with chic navy leather and blue Venetian glass to create a stylish yet cosy atmosphere in which to enjoy the extensive brasserie-style menu (rabbit in beer sauce, horse steak with *frites*, beef *carbonnade*) served by white-aproned waiters.

Le Fin de Siècle 16

R. de l'Armée 3

✆ 732 7434

🚇 Metro Montgomery or trams 81 and 82

Open: Mon–Fri 1200–1430, 1900–2230, Sat 1900–2230

Reservations essential

No credit cards accepted

A wonderfully romantic Italian restaurant, with dark burgundy-coloured dining rooms, rich velvet drapes, candles and classical music, an imaginative menu of fresh pastas and salads, and a decent choice of Italian wines. If you can't get in here, there's a second branch at av. Louise 423 (✆ *648 8041*).

L'Horloge du Sud ⑰

R. du Trône 141

✆ 512 1864

🚍 Buses 34, 38, 60, 80, 95 and 96

Open: café: Mon–Fri 1100–0100, Sat–Sun 1700–0100; food: 1200–1430, 1900–2400

No credit cards accepted

You'll hear all sorts of languages and dialects spoken in this multi-cultural café-bar on the fringes of Matongué, the African quarter of the city. The unusual menu features an impressive choice of rums from around the world and a handful of classic dishes from Africa and South America: try the spiced green bananas in a rich coconut-butter sauce or the more substantial pan-fried fish with palm-nut sauce, fried plantains and cassava leaves.

James Joyce ⑱

R. Archimède 34

✆ 230 9894

🚇 Metro Schuman or bus 22

Open: Mon–Fri 1100–0130, Sat–Sun 1200–0130

All credit cards accepted

Of all the Irish pubs in the EU quarter, this is the most authentic (and one of the most boisterous). Happy hour runs from 1800 until 1900 and there is occasional traditional folk music in the evenings, a beer garden and hearty pub food served all day.

Le Jardin de Nicolas ⑲

Av. de Tervuren 137

✆ 732 2449

🚇 Metro Montgomery or trams 81 and 82

Open: daily 1000–0100

Small, cramped and rather hectic, this *in-*

brasserie attracts a young crowd for its steak-*frites*, salads, pastas and varied choice of beers. There are tables outside, set back from the main road, in summer.

Poivre et Sel ⑳

R. Parnasse 2

✆ 503 4693

🚇 Metro Trône

Open: Mon–Fri 1130–1500, 1800–2200

Reservations recommended

All credit cards accepted

Italian cuisine with a twist, with such favourites as carpaccio of pigeon with balsamic vinegar and cannelloni filled with salmon mousse on the menu, served in a rustic, yellow-and-white conservatory-style restaurant, with an open kitchen and a jolly atmosphere, or under parasols on the pavement outside.

Takesushi ㉑

Blvd Charlemagne 21

✆ 230 5627

🚇 Metro Schuman

Open: Mon–Fri 1200–1430, 1900–2230, Sun 1800–2230

All credit cards accepted

The inauspicious façade belies an atmospheric Japanese restaurant and garden terrace, hugely popular with Eurocrats, who come for the good-value sushi lunch menu, the delicious *sashimi* and traditional hot dishes too.

EU DISTRICT
Shops, markets and picnic sites

Shops

La Crèmerie Cachée 22

Pl. Jourdan 37

Buses 34, 59 and 80

Open: Mon–Tue and Thu–Fri 0900–2000, Sat–Sun 0900–1900

No credit cards accepted

A traditional cheese shop selling a splendid selection of Belgian, French, Spanish and Swiss cheeses, many of which are produced on small-scale farms, and then further matured in the shop's cellar. Among the tastiest Belgian cheeses on offer are Herve, Le Bailli, Orval and Pas de Bleu. There is also a choice selection of pâtés, jams, pickles, sauces and wines.

Aux Délices de Capoue 23

Av. des Celtes 36

Trams 81 and 82

Open: daily 1200–2200

No credit cards accepted

Ice-cream fanatics come from far and wide to taste the delicious ice creams here. There are over forty different flavours to choose from, including old favourites (vanilla, chocolate, strawberry) together with more exotic flavours – cinnamon,

speculoos (caramelised biscuit), marzipan and *quark* (*fromage blanc*) – and tart grapefruit, cherry, lemon and gooseberry sorbets.

Le Fermier 24

R. Archimède 59

Metro Schuman or bus 22

Open: Mon–Fri 0900–1900, Sat 0900–1500

The scent of sweet ripe peaches, apricots and melons lures you into this small Italian-owned delicatessen, brimming with fresh pasta, different pestos, olive oils, vinegars, cheeses, cold cuts and wines from Italy.

Mi-Figue Mi-Raisin 25

R. Archimède 71

Metro Schuman or bus 22

Open: Mon–Fri 0800–1900, Sat 0800–1300.

No credit cards accepted

A popular patisserie near the Berlaimont Centre, selling delicious organic bread, cakes, quiches, waffles and salads to take away or to enjoy in the garden at the back of the shop.

Neuhaus 26

R. Archimède 35

Metro Schuman or bus 22

Open: Mon–Fri 0900–1830, Sat 0930–1300.

All credit cards accepted

Jean Neuhaus, one of the world's best-known names in chocolate, invented the legendary *praline* (a chocolate with a filling inside) in 1912. Today the company boasts over seventy different types of handmade pralines, and this particular branch caters mainly for sweet-toothed Eurocrats.

Le Pain Quotidien 27

R. du Luxembourg 68

Metro Trône

Open: Mon–Fri 0730–2000

All credit cards accepted

The EU branch of a growing chain of country-kitchen-style bakeries, serving delicious cakes, sandwiches, snacks and pastries. There's also a pavement terrace on which to linger over a cup of coffee, whilst watching local politicians at play in the numerous bars and cafés flanking lively place du Luxembourg.

Savour Club 28

Pl. St-Pierre 38

Buses 34, 59 and 89

Open: Mon–Sat 1000–1900

All credit cards accepted

You'll find a surprisingly large choice of classic wines from around the globe in this small *cave de Bruxelles*, together with knowledgeable staff and a useful wine revue to assist you with your purchases.

Au Vatel 29

Pl. Jourdan 27

🚊 Buses 34, 59 and 80

Open: 24 hours a day, closed Wed

All credit cards accepted

The best thing about this long-established bakery, apart from its mouth-watering gateaux, its ice-cream cakes and its novelty animal-shaped loaves, is that it is open 24 hours a day.

Markets

Place Jourdan 30

🚊 Buses 34, 59 and 80

Open: Sun 0800–1400

Join the locals of this increasingly fashionable residential quarter in their weekly purchase of fruit, vegetables, cheeses and cold cuts from this Sunday morning market.

Picnic sites

Parc du Cinquantenaire 31

🚇 Metro Schuman or Merode

Although Brussels was willing to sacrifice the core of a beautiful 19th-century residential district to build the European Parliament and European Commission and all their administrative offices here, it has no intention of destroying its parks. Indeed, after Washington, Brussels has more green spaces than any other city in the world, and this one is probably the most famous, created in 1880 to celebrate fifty years of Belgian independence. The monumental buildings at its heart contain a variety of museums (art, history, cars, military history, etc) and an elegant café serving snacks, salads and sandwiches, and all around are regal lawns, populated by lovers, picnickers, children and joggers.

Parc Léopold 32

R. Belliard

🚇 Metro Maelbeek or buses 21, 54 and 59

When in Brussels do as the Eurocrats do, grab a sandwich from **Arthur's Café** nearby (*r. Trèves 26; ∅ 503 8937; open: Mon–Fri 0730–1700*) and enjoy your lunch hour beside the lake in this tiny green oasis alongside the metal and glass European Parliament buildings.

Square Ambiorix 33

R. Archimède

🚊 Buses 22, 29, 54 and 63

The largest of three leafy squares (together with Square Marguerite to the west and Square Marie-Louise to the east) providing welcome respite from the traffic-choked boulevards of the European quarter. In fine weather, there's even a small van on the corner of r. Archimède selling ice creams and waffles.

Business restaurants

Dining to impress

Not only is Brussels the capital of Europe, it is also the capital of European gastronomy and, with a staggering 1 800-plus restaurants to choose from, there's no shortage of top-notch eateries for business entertaining. Belgium has more gourmet restaurants per capita than France – even the French admit that Belgian cuisine ranks among the best in Europe – and Brussels enjoys more Michelin-rated restaurants than Paris.

Two restaurants at the dizzying pinnacle of haute cuisine have been awarded the ultimate accolade – three Michelin stars. Pierre Wynant at **Comme Chez Soi** in the city centre (*pl. Rouppe 23; ∅ 512 2921; closed Sun and Mon; booking essential; jacket and tie required;* ❶❷❸) is currently considered Belgium's greatest modern chef, and one of the most celebrated in Europe. Over the years, not only has he reintroduced traditional ingredients such as beer and hop shoots back on to Belgian menus, but he has also transformed the reputation of his country's hearty country-style cuisine into a refined and subtle nouvelle *Bruxelloise* cuisine. The second gourmet temple is **Bruneau** in the northwestern suburb of Ganshoren (*av. Broustin 75; ∅ 427 6978; closed Tue evening and Wed; booking essential; jacket and tie required;* ❶❷❸), Jean-Pierre Bruneau's luxurious restaurant, highly acclaimed for its inventive French haute cuisine, with prices to match.

A handful of Bruxellois restaurants have been awarded two Michelin

▲ Atrium, Hotel Radisson

stars, including **Claude Dupont** (*av. Vital-Rietuisen 46; ✆ 426 0000; closed Mon and Tue; booking essential;* ❸❸❸), a long-established restaurant which offers excellent-value 3-, 5- and 7-course menus, and the Radisson Hotel's **Sea Grill** (*see page 21*), one of Brussels' top seafood restaurants.

Some of the most popular venues for a business lunch or dinner are within the various hotels about town. Apart from the Sea Grill, there's also the **Atrium** at the Radisson (*r. du Fossé-aux-Loups 47; ✆ 227 3170;* ❸❸), a smart café in the vast lobby area which is handy for a sandwich or a snack if you're rushed. Or try **La Maison du Boeuf** at the Hilton (one Michelin star, *see page 61*) for a full-blown gourmet meal overlooking Parc d'Egmont. The stylish five-star **Stanhope-Brighton** restaurant (*see page 51*) is popular for its four-course business menu at midday, while **Les 4 Seasons** (*r. de l'Home Chrêtian 2; ✆ 505 5100; closed Sat lunch and Sun evening; booking essential;* ❸❸❸), discreetly lodged on the first floor of centrally placed Hotel Windsor, offers a fortnightly changing, 3-course business lunch, which is reasonably priced and includes wine.

No matter which part of the capital, you'll find most of the gastronomic restaurants are frequented by the city's 'elite' – EU movers and shakers, diplomats and businessmen. It is always advisable to reserve a table in advance, especially at lunchtimes. Over a dozen restaurants have one Michelin star and are always fully booked. They include **La Truffe Noire** (*see page 71*), celebrated for its truffle-based cuisine; top fish restaurant **L'Écailler du Palais Royal** (*see page 38*); sumptuous **Villa Lorraine** (*Chaussée de la Hulpe 28; ✆ 347 3163; closed Sun; booking essential;* ❸❸❸), frequented by the 'beautiful people' and serving traditional French and Bruxellois cuisine on the edge of the Bois de la Cambre in Uccles; and **Les Baguetes Imperiales** in the northwestern suburb of Laeken (*av. Jean Sobieski; ✆ 479 6732; closed Sun evening and Tue; booking essential;* ❸❸❸), Belgium's only Michelin-starred oriental restaurant, which specialises in exquisite Vietnamese cuisine.

If you want to mix with the Eurocrats, head for the Etterbeek district where, unsurprisingly, there is a glut of fine restaurants. **Atelier Européen** (*see page 48*) is especially favoured by politicians, diplomats, lawyers and journalists for its sensational help-yourself lunchtime buffet. For those looking for a light bite and a pint between meetings, there are also several lively pubs in the area, including Irish pubs **Kitty O'Sheas** (*blvd Charlemagne 42; ✆ 230 7875;* ❸) and **The Wild Geese** (*av. Livingstone 2–4; ✆ 230 1990;* ❸).

> **If you want to mix with the Eurocrats, head for the Etterbeek district where, unsurprisingly, there is a glut of fine restaurants.**

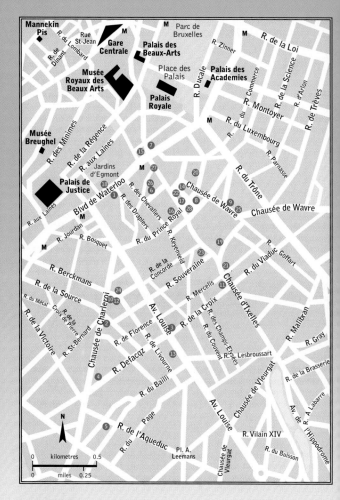

Mannekin Pis ◆

R. du Lombard

Rue St-Jean

M

Gare Centrale

R. de Dinant

Musée Royaux des Beaux Arts ■

Palais des Beaux-Arts

M

Parc de Bruxelles

R. Zinner

M

R. de la Loi

Place des Palais

Palais Royale

R. Ducale

Palais des Academies

R. du Commerce

R. Montoyer

R. de la Science

R. d'Arlon

R. de Trèves

Musée Breughel ■

R. des Minimes

R. de la Régence

R. aux Laines

M

R. du Luxembourg

R. Parnasse

(15)

(7)

Jardins d'Egmont

(27)

M

(20)

R. du Trône

Palais de Justice

Blvd de Waterloo

(18)

(26)

(6)

(14)

Chaussée de Wavre

(12)

(22)

R. des Chevaliers

R. des Drapiers

(16)

(17)

(28)

(9)

(25)

R. aux Laines

R. Jourdan

R. Bosquet

R. du Prince Royal

R. Keyenveld

Chaussée de Wavre

M

R. Berckmans

R. de la Source

R. du Métal

Croix de Pierre

R. de la

R. St-Bernard

R. de la Victoire

Chaussée de Charleroi

(24)

(10)

(12)

(2)

Av. Louise

R. de Florence

R. de Livourne

R. Defacqz

R. du Bailli

R. Page

(3)

(13)

R. de la Concorde

R. Souveraine

R. Mercelis

R. de la Croix

R. des Champs-Elysées

R. du Couvent

(23)

(19)

(21)

(11)

Chaussée d'Ixelles

R. du Viaduc Goffart

Lesbroussart

R. Malibran

R. Gray

R. de la Brasserie

(5)

R. de l'Aqueduc

Pl. A. Leemans

Av. Louise

Chaussée de Vleurgat

Chaussée de Vleurgat

R. Vilain XIV

R. du Buisson

Av. de l'Hippodrome

Av. A. Labarre

N

0 ——— kilometres ——— 0.5
0 ——— miles ——— 0.25

Louise

The Louise district stretches from the city's main shopping zone in the west with its glamorous shops, up-market cafés and restaurants around avenue Louise, through the trendy quarter of Saint-Boniface, with its art-nouveau bars and bistros populated by a young laid-back crowd, to vibrant Matongé in the east, the African quarter of town.

LOUISE
Restaurants

Adrienne ❶

R. Capitaine Crespel 1a

Ø 511 9339

Ⓜ Metro Louise or bus 34 or trams 91, 92, 93 and 94

Open: Mon–Sat 1200–1400, 1830–2200, Sun 1130–1400

Reservations recommended

All credit cards accepted

International

❸❸❸

There's a dazzling array of dishes here: fish, *fruits de mer*, crustaceans, cold meats, pâtés, terrines and salads, not to mention the separate table of cheeses and desserts. Excellent value for money and especially popular for Sunday brunch.

Amadeus ❷

R. Veydt 13

Ø 538 3427

Ⓜ Trams 91 and 92

Open: daily 1830–0100

Reservations recommended (Reservations essential for Sun brunch)

All credit cards accepted

Belgian

❸❸

One of the capital's most atmospheric restaurants and wine bars contained in the one-time studio of Auguste Rodin. The food is Belgian, both traditional and modern, with a typical menu including carpaccio, caramelised spare ribs, guinea fowl with juniper berries, several vegetarian options and the house speciality *waterzooi*, rounded off by a selection of homemade tarts. Make sure you reserve a table for the eat-as-much-as-you-want Sunday brunch (*1000–1400*)!

The Avenue ❸

Av. Louise 156

Ø 253 5456

Ⓜ Trams 93 and 94

Open: Tue–Sat 1000–2200

Reservations recommended

All credit cards accepted

French

❸❸❸

The Avenue is housed in a stylish conversion of a city mansion into a suitably sophisticated restaurant complex. On the top floor there's the cool sage-green and white Avenue Restaurant, a gastronomic *tour de force* presided over by the celebrated chef, Andre d'Haese. On the ground floor **The White Room** offers special tastings, private receptions and a tea salon. In the basement the **Gastroshop** is perhaps the most striking element of the ensemble. It's actually *in* the restaurant kitchens.

Bar Bar Sol ❹

R. Defacqz 105

Ø 534 6855

Ⓜ Trams 81, 82, 91 and 92

Open: Mon–Wed 1100–1430, 1900–2300, Thu–Sat 1100–1430, 1900–2400, closed Sat lunch

Reservations essential

All credit cards accepted

French (Provençal)

❸❸❸

Start your meal with pasta and tapenade sauce (made with anchovies and capers), followed by fillet of red

Restaurant avec jardin

Bar Bar Sol

Rue Defacqz, 105   Tél et Fax 534.68.55
1050 Bruxelles   Fermé samedi midi et dimanche

mullet *à la niçoise* (with tomatoes and olives). The wine list is a little disappointing – no Provençal wines – but there's a good selection from other regions of France.

Le Bison Teint ⑤

R. de l'Acqueduct 63

✆ 534 9584

🚊 Trams 81 and 82 or bus 54

Open: Mon–Sat 1900–2300 (2400 Fri–Sat)

Reservations recommended

💳 💳

French

💷💷–💷💷💷

The patron here comes from Besançon in France where the inhabitants are known as 'les Bisontins', hence the strange name, Le Bison Teint (The Tinted Bison). Don't expect bison on the menu, although you may find ostrich, kangaroo and even llama from time to time. There's a good variety of salads, steaks, fondues and fish dishes on the menu, and *raclette* (potatoes served with special hot, runny cheese) evenings are held every Monday and Tuesday.

Les Jardins de Bagatelle ⑥

R. du Berger 17

✆ 512 1276

🚇 Metro Porte de Namur or buses 54 and 71

Open: Mon–Sat 1200–1430, 1900–2230, closed Sat lunch

Reservations recommended

All credit cards accepted

Fusion

💷💷💷

Everything here is a little eccentric. The restaurant is decorated in such bright reds, golds and blues you almost need sunglasses when you walk in. Add to this some exotic plants, flamboyant drapes, leopard-skin seats, African music and art-works by local artists and you start to get the picture. The menu is equally wacky – pre-dominantly French but dotted with African and Asian specialities.

La Maison du Boeuf

Hilton Hotel, blvd de Waterloo 38

✆ 504 2111

🚇 Metro Louise or bus 34 or trams 91, 92, 93 and 94

Open: daily 1200–1430, 1900–2230

Reservations recommended

All credit cards accepted

French

❶❶❶

In the kitchen head chef, Michel Theurel, is a *maître cuisinier* of Belgium, a disciple of Escoffier, the world-renowned Flemish chef, and president of the Culinary Academy of France. In the stylish restaurant overlooking Parc d' Egmont, the *maître d'hôtel* was the premier *sommelier* of Belgium a few years back. Their combined skills, and a menu of imaginative but not fussy French cuisine, guarantee you a meal to remember.

Saint-Boniface ❽

R. St-Boniface 9

✆ 511 5366

🚇 Buses 54 and 71

Open: Mon–Sat 1200–1430, 1900–2200, closed Sat lunch

Reservations recommended lunchtimes and eves at weekend

All credit cards accepted

French

❶❶

The menu here is hard to resist: hot goats' cheese with duck breast in pastry; mushroom caps stuffed with snails; tripe simmered slowly in champagne; hot Lyonnais sausage on a bed of warm potato salad; tarte Tatin, mar-quise of chocolate with an apricot coulis …

La Scala ❾

Chaussée de Wavre 132

✆ 514 4995

🚇 Buses 54 and 71

Open: Mon–Sat 1200–1430, 1900–2200, closed Sat lunch

Reservations recommended

All credit cards accepted

Italian

❶❶❶

Dress smartly for this sophisticated Italian two-storey restaurant, with its refined menu

(including lobster ravioli with basil and saffron sauce, salmon in lemon butter, and nougat *glacée*) and elegant sur-rounds. On Fridays and Saturday nights, a pianist sets the scene for a romantic dinner in the ground-floor restaurant.

Tierra del Fuego ❿

R. Berckmans 14

✆ 537 4272

🚇 Trams 91, 92, 93 and 94

Open: 1830–0030 (Fri–Sun 0200)

Reservations recommended

VISA 💳 American Express

Latin American

❶❶

At this great restaurant the décor is bright and exotic, the menu hot and spicy (chilli con carne, enchiladas, grilled prawns in lemon sauce, mixed *tapas*), and there's a lovely candlelit garden with fountains and Gaudí-style seating. Try the Latin American cocktails, the different rums and coffees. There's even a cabinet of cigars from Havana to complete a thor-oughly enjoyable meal.

Les Jardins de Bagatelle
RESTAURANT - TRAITEUR

LOUISE
Bars, cafés and pubs

L'Amour Fou ⑪

Chaussée d'Ixelles 185

✆ 514 2709

🚌 Buses 54 and 71

Open: Mon–Fri 0900–0100, Sat–Sun 1000–0200

All credit cards accepted

💶

This relaxed locals' bar attracts a young, laid-back crowd – for coffee and croissant to start the day; for steak-*frites*, chilli or a hearty dollop of *stoemp* at mealtimes; or to read the local newspapers (found hanging about on wooden sticks) over a glass of beer. Wine is served by the pitcher or by the centimetre, and crayons and drawing blocks are provided to keep the kids amused.

L'Autre Ailleurs ⑫

R. Berckmans 2

✆ 538 1023

🚋 Trams 91, 92, 93 and 94

Open: Mon–Fri 1200–1430, 1900–2230

💳 American Express

💶💶

A small, beautiful restaurant decorated in cool black and grey and illuminated by candles. The menu combines French and Italian cuisine, with such dishes as duck with caramelised onions, honey and ginger, and ravioli with salmon and saffron. Be sure to save room for the chocolate tart!

Caprices d'Ambiance ⑬

Av. Louise 173

✆ 649 9474

🚋 Trams 81, 82 93 and 94 or bus 54

Open: Mon–Wed 1200–1500, Thu–Sat 1200–1500, 1900–2300

💳 💶

💶💶

A recently opened restaurant with a young chef who is just 25. On one level there are snacks and sandwiches, while in the tranquil cream, baroque-style dining room you will be treated to a menu of elegant meat and fish dishes, gently perfumed with fresh herbs and spices. The wine list is short but classic and, behind the restaurant, there is a small, slightly unkempt garden.

Le Chantecler ⑭

Chaussée de Wavre 47

✆ 512 4378

🚇 Metro Porte de Namur or buses 54 and 71

Open: daily 1200–1500, 1800–2300

💳 💶 American Express

💶💶

One of the oldest restaurants in the district, whose speciality is mussels. Initially it served nothing but mussels, with 45 different sauces. Now they serve just a dozen preparations (with lemon, in lobster bisque, in champagne, with red wine, celery and tomatoes) and also a good selection of pasta dishes and pizzas cooked in a wood-oven.

La Paniscia 15

R. de la Reinette 4

✆ 513 4915

Ⓜ Metro Porte de Namur or buses 34, 54 and 71

Open: Mon–Fri 1200–1430, 1900–2230

All credit cards accepted

Ⓒ Ⓒ Ⓒ

This small, refined restaurant is devoted to the cuisine of the Piedmont region of Italy. Try the ravioli *con fonduta* (a regional cheese), mixed *antipasti* and the fillet of lamb cooked in Barbera (a local wine) and truffles, followed by the succulent almond and hazelnut tart. Reserve a table in advance.

Le Requin Chagrin 16

R. du Prince Royal 11

✆ 512 2686

Ⓑ Buses 54 and 71

Open: Tue–Sat 1200–1400, 1930–2200

All credit cards accepted

Ⓒ Ⓒ

A sophisticated orange and dark green décor,

cane and bamboo, tropical plants and rhythmic creole music all fuse to create an exotic atmosphere at 'The Sad Shark', a restaurant and rum-bar, specialising in dishes from the island of La Réunion. Fish reigns supreme on the menu, served with lime and spices, with coconut, or ginger and sugar cane sauce. Meat dishes include duck with papaya and sweet peppers. Booking is highly recommended, especially at weekends.

Saveurs du Sud 17

R. St-Boniface 34

✆ 502 7743

Ⓑ Buses 54 and 71

Open: Mon–Sat 1200–1500, 1900–2300, closed Sat lunch

Ⓒ Ⓒ

You're sure to forget all stereotypical images of Greek restaurants when you enter into this calm, uncluttered café in trendy rue Saint-Boniface with its blue-wood garden furniture and sunny yellow walls. The menu is equally pleasing – plain, honest home-cooking with all the old favourites: stuffed vine leaves, moussaka, *stifado*, feta salads, and gooey Greek yoghurt with honey to round off a simple but perfect meal.

Saxe Café 18

Blvd de Waterloo 49

✆ 511 5090

Ⓜ Metro Louise or bus 34 or trams 91, 92, 93 and 94

Open: closed Mon eve, Sat lunch and Sun

All credit cards accepted

Ⓒ Ⓒ

Wedged between such designers as Gucci, Ferragamo and Versace on the boulevard de Waterloo, Saxe Café is undeniably stylish, with a minimalist interior of wood and terracotta tones. Even the menu follows the latest trend, that of 'fusion' food, combining French, Italian and Thai. A great people-watching venue, especially at weekends or on Tuesday nights when there's live jazz.

Sounds 19

R. de la Tulipe 28

✆ 512 9250

Ⓑ Buses 54 and 71

Open: Mon–Fri 1130–0400, Sat 1900–0400

No credit cards accepted

Ⓒ

A small, homely café and jazz-concert venue near place Fernand Cocq, staging live jazz sessions four or five times a week and the occasional Latino night when you can tango the night away with the locals. Check out their website for concert details: *www.cyclone.be/ sounds*.

L'Ultime Atome 14

R. St-Boniface 14

✆ 511 1367

Ⓑ Buses 54 and 71

Open: daily 0830–2400

€

In the shadow of the imposing Gothic pile of Saint-Boniface Church, this trendy, modern café is always buzzing. People come here to relax, to meet friends, to chat, to eat, to sit on the pavement-terrace and watch passers-by and to try out one of the 85 beers on offer. Food is typically bistro-style, with daily changing specials, a kitchen which remains open all day, and more vegetarian options than usual.

Vie Sauvage ㉑

R. de Naples 12

Ø 513 6885

🚌 Buses 54 and 71

Open: Tue–Sun 1200–1400, 1930–2300, closed Sat lunch and Sun lunch

No credit cards accepted

€€

A large Moroccan restaurant with aromatic cuisine (*tagines*, grills and kebabs) to match the spicy tones of the décor with its terracotta coloured walls, mosaic-tiled tables and multi-coloured lanterns. Add to this an open fire, candlelight, a lawned garden, Moroccan music and wine, and a variety of intimate nooks and crannies, and you have the perfect recipe for an intimate evening.

Volle Gas ㉑

Pl. Fernand Cocq 12

Ø 502 8917

🚌 Buses 54 and 71

Open: Mon–Sat 1100–0100, Sun 1800–0100

All credit cards accepted

€

Situated on the corner of a grassy square, this bustling brasserie is popular with all ages, thanks to its comprehensive list of beers and its reliable menu of Belgian staples, including braised endives, rabbit with Kriek beer, beef *carbonnade*, *waterzooi*, mussels in season and ubiquitous sausage and *stoemp*. The venue was formerly a jazz bar called the Bierodrome and there is still live jazz here a few times each month. In spring and summer there is a pavement terrace.

Yamato ㉒

R. Francart 11

Ø 502 2893

🚌 Buses 54 and 71

Open: Tue–Sat 1200–1400, 1900–2200 (Sat 1830–2130)

Reservations not allowed

American Express

€

This tiny noodle bar on the corner of rue Francart and rue Saint-Boniface is hugely popular and, as there are just 16 seats around a central wooden counter, you must be prepared to wait before you can tuck into your *miso* soup, *gyoza* (Japanese ravioli) and noodles. Most of the clientele are Japanese – either suited business-men working in Brussels, or young students reading Japanese comics – which is always a good sign.

Yamayu-Santatsu ㉓

Chaussée d'Ixelles 141

Ø 513 5312

🚌 Buses 54 and 71

Open: daily 1200–1400, 1900–2215

American Express

€€

This small, minimalist Japanese restaurant is the oldest in Brussels, and also one of the most authentic. The sushi and *sashimi* are especially good – made before your very eyes if you sit at the main counter.

LOUISE
Shops, markets and picnic sites

Shops

Aromes et Délices

R. Berckmans 1a

Ⓜ Trams 91, 92, 93 and 94

Open: Mon 1000–1400, Tue–Fri 1000–1900, Sat 1045–1830

All credit cards accepted

This tiny wine-merchants' specialises exclusively in fine wines from France, together with a choice selection of champagnes and cigars.

Beer Mania 25

Chaussée de Wavre 174–6

Ⓜ Buses 54 and 71

Open: daily 1100–1900

An absolute must for beer fanatics, this small shop sells over four hundred different Belgian beers. As drinking beer is something of an art form here, they also stock all their respective glasses, as well as combined bottle-and-glass gift packages. And, should you miss the taste of Belgian beer once you leave the country, they have a website for home orders and international deliveries: *www.beermania.be*.

Le Comptoir Florian 14

R. St-Boniface 17

Ⓜ Buses 54 and 71

Open: Tue–Sat 1100–2000

No credit cards accepted

Fancy a cuppa? You'll receive a warm welcome at this small art-nouveau shop (designed by Blérot, one of the city's leading 19th-century architects), where you can taste and purchase huge varieties of teas from around the globe.

Coté Vaisselle 26

R. Stassart 46

Ⓜ Metro Porte de Namur or buses 34, 54 and 71

Open: Mon–Sat 1000–1830

All credit cards accepted

If you're weary of the same old kitchenware, splash out in this veritable treasure trove of pots and pans, baskets and trays, porcelain, glass, pottery and table linen, all at unbeatable prices.

Leonidas 27

Chaussée d'Ixelles 5

Ⓜ Metro Porte de Namur or buses 34, 54 and 71

Open: daily 0900–1830

No credit cards accepted

Leonidas are the best-selling pralines in Belgium – possibly because of their unique selling concept: most of their shops have a counter opening on to the street.

Le Tartisan 28

R. St-Boniface 4

Ⓜ Buses 54 and 71

Open: Mon–Fri 1000–1900, Sat 1000–1830

In this small delicatessen, chef and owner Marc Lejeune prepares the sweetest of tarts and the tastiest of quiches which he will willingly heat up for you to eat on the spot.

Seasonal cuisine

Brussels sprouts, hop shoots, herrings, venison …

Belgian cuisine is built on a solid foundation of fresh market produce of the highest quality. It is a simple style of cooking, healthy, plain and firmly rooted in a peasant tradition, which relies heavily on seafood, substantial stews and vegetables, and which changes with the seasons.

Belgium is especially well known for its **vegetables**. Since the 14th century it has been considered the 'vegetable garden' of Europe, one of the first countries to mass-produce fresh vegetables, and still today the largest exporter in Europe. It was the Belgians who introduced the carrot and the turnip to Britain, and who developed many new types of vegetables including chicory (*chicon*), hop shoots (*jets de houblon*) and, of course, Brussels sprouts (*choux de Bruxelles*).

Hop shoots are one of the most popular springtime vegetables, cooked in cream with a pinch of nutmeg, or poached with eggs, fish, white meat or sweetbreads. Another spring staple is **asparagus**. From May onwards nearly every restaurant has a special asparagus menu. It is served in a wide variety of sauces, but the most typically Belgian way to cook it is with butter, hard-boiled egg and chive. Two good bar restaurants for hop shoot dishes and asparagus in season are **La Grande Porte** (*see page 43*) and **Aux Armes de Bruxelles** (*see page 9*).

Another springtime favourite is the **common shrimp** (*crevettes gris*), netted by fishermen on the North Sea coast the old-fashioned way – on horseback at low tide, following a tradition that dates back to the 1400s. These tiny shrimps are served in salads, in stuffed tomatoes or made into scrumptious croquettes, coated with breadcrumbs and deep-fried till crisp. They are a great speciality at **La Taverne du Passage** (*see page 11*).

Spring is also the time for new potatoes, baby carrots, leeks, green beans, and salads. *Salade liégeoise* (a warm salad of green

▲ Place du Châtelein market

beans) is one favourite. It's also the season of the first goats' cheeses. Trout and salmon are in abundance, and *anguilles au vert* features frequently on the menu – eel cooked in a green herb sauce made with chervil, sorrel and parsley.

In early summer **herrings** (*maatjes*), fresh from the North Sea, become a prominent part of the seasonal cuisine. Try them in any of the seafood restaurants around **place Sainte-Catherine** (*see pages 29-31*). Salads are also popular in summer months, with fresh garden herbs, goats' cheeses and Ardennes ham. It's the picnic season too, so pâtés, terrines, quiches and wholesome country loaves come to the fore in delicatessens, and puddings (yoghurts, ice creams, sorbets, tarts) become predominantly fruit-based, thanks to the abundance of cherries, strawberries, apricots, rhubarb and gooseberries.

By the time autumn lowers the temperatures, everybody's favourite – *moules-frites* – is once more widely available after its summer break (the mussel season runs from September to April). Autumn also heralds the season of mushrooms, celeriac, courgettes, aubergines and Brussels sprouts, and from mid-October game begins to feature on the menus of traditional Bruxellois restaurants, with pheasant, pigeon, venison and hare often served with raisins or wild berries. **Au Brabançon** (*r. de la Commune 75; ✆ 217 7191; ❸❸❸*), one of Belgium's most fashionable traditional-style restaurants, recently awarded the Grand Prix de la Cuisine Artisanale de Régionale, has a particularly impressive seasonal game menu.

Winter is welcomed with a more hearty fare of soups, sausages, black pudding (*bloed-pens*), sauerkraut and *stoemp*. Stews come to the fore, including *waterzooi* (chicken with leeks, parsley and cream sauce), *lapin à la gueuze* (rabbit stewed in beer) and *carbonnade flamande* (*see recipe on page 94*). Chicory (*chicon*) is one of the more popular winter vegetables, braised gently with butter, lemon juice, brown sugar and nutmeg, or wrapped in slices of ham and baked in a cheese sauce (*chicon gratin*). Desserts too become more nourishing, including such dishes as pears poached in cherry beer, *tarte Tatin*, crème brûlée with Orval beer, and rich chocolate gateaux. To try some of the beer-based dishes, visit **In't Spinnekopke** (*see pages 26 and 30*). For other seasonal delights, **Le Petit Pont** (*r. du Doyenne 114-16; ✆ 346 4949; closed Mon-Tue; ❸❸*), **Bermuchet** (*r. Haute 198; ✆ 513 8882; closed Sat-Sun lunch; ❸❸*) and **Au Stekerlapatte** (*see page 26*) are all recommended for their *cuisine traditionnelle belge*.

> **These tiny shrimps are served in salads, in stuffed tomatoes or made into scrumptious croquettes, coated with breadcrumbs and deep-fried till crisp.**

Ixelles

Ixelles is one of the city's most attractive and atmospheric communes. Primarily a residential district, its elegant squares and hilly, twisting streets shelter a plethora of fashionable restaurants and brasseries, and the student quarter to the south is a constant hive of activity with its lively and affordable bistros, cafés and bars open late into the night.

IXELLES
Restaurants

Bistrot du Mail ①

R. du Mail 81

∅ 539 0697

⦿ Buses 54 and 60 or trams 81 and 82

Open: Mon–Sat 1200–1430, 1900–2300, closed Sat lunch

Reservations essential

All credit cards accepted

French

●●●

This cosy terracotta and navy-blue restaurant offers a small but seductive menu, with daily changing suggestions based on the freshest of market produce. The four-course *menu de marché* is especially good value, with such dishes as tuna tartare, grilled sole salad with herb vinaigrette and rabbit with rosemary and caramelised fennel.

Brasseries Georges ②

Av. Winston Churchill 259

∅ 347 2100

⦿ Bus 38 or trams 23 and 90

Open: daily 1130–0030 (Fri–Sat 0100)

Reservations recommended

All credit cards accepted

French

●●●

With this brasserie's gleaming brass-work, its dark-wood panelling, mirrors and stained glass, its bustling atmosphere and its waiters in long white aprons, you would be forgiven for thinking you were in Paris. The menu comprises such classics as *cassoulet*,

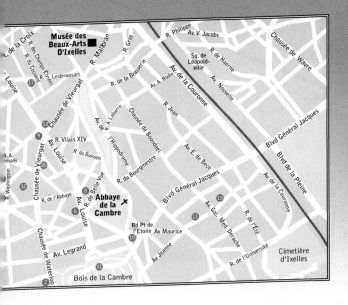

sauerkraut, and *andouillettes*. There are daily specials scribbled on a blackboard, an excellent beer and wine list and, outside on the terrace, the shellfish counter is reputedly one of the finest in Brussels.

Fellini ❸

Pl. du Châtelein 32

Ø 534 4549

🚍 Bus 54 or trams 81 and 82

Open: Mon–Sat 1200–1500, 1900–2400, closed Sat lunch

Reservations recommended

All credit cards accepted

Italian

❷❷

The highly original décor of this two-storey restaurant is based on the atmospheric railway station in the Fellini film *8½*, with its metal and brass girders, its large clock, its suspended lamps and wooden railway-carriage seating. The voguish menu includes such pasta dishes as square spaghetti with goose livers, tagliatelle with smoked salmon and vodka, and there is usually a good selection of vegetarian dishes.

O' comme 3 Pommes ❹

Pl. du Châtelein 40

Ø 644 0323

🚍 Bus 54 or trams 81 and 82

Open: Mon–Sat 1200–1430, 1900–2230, closed Sat lunch and Mon lunch

Reservations essential

🔲 💳 American Express

French

❸❸❸

The name *O' comme 3 pommes* means 'knee-high to a grasshopper' – an appropriate description for this tiny, modern restaurant, with its elegant green, yellow and white décor which revolves around an apple (*pomme*) theme. The cooking is essentially French, but with Italian and Asian influences that result in such unusual combinations as turbot with mango and coriander, or liver

▲ Brasseries Georges

poached on a bed of rhubarb. Apples feature frequently on the menu too. Try the *tarte Tatin* of smoked duck and apple!

Les Perles de Pluie ⑤

R. du Châtelein 25

☎ 649 6723

🚊 Bus 54 or trams 81 and 82

Open: Tue–Sun 1200–1500, 1900–2200, closed Sat lunch

Reservations recommended

All credit cards accepted

Thai

❸❸❸

Sumptuously decorated with Thai furnishings, drapes and exotic plants, there's even a small 'Buddhist temple' room where you can enjoy an aperitif to the sounds of the *gamalan*. Choose from a variety of reasonably priced menus or opt for the extensive à la carte which combines such classics as *tom kha gai* and beef satay with other more unusual dishes. Undoubtedly the best value of all is the sensational Sunday brunch (*1200–2300*).

La Porte des Indes ⑥

Av. Louise 455

☎ 374 4962

🚊 Trams 93 and 94

Open: daily 1200–1430, 1900–2230

Reservations essential

All credit cards accepted

Indian

❷❷–❷❷❷

'The Gate of India' is without doubt a cut above your average curry house, with its sumptuous, candlelit dining room of exotic fabrics and spicy Eastern colours evocative of a Maharajah's palace. This is very much a dining experience for those who love Indian food but who are tired of formula curries, and are prepared to pay for the palate-expanding experience.

La Quincaillerie ⑦

R. du Page 45

☎ 538 2553

🚊 Buses 54 and 60 or trams 81 and 82

Open: daily 1200–1430, 1900–2400, closed Sat lunch and Sun lunch

Reservations essential

All credit cards accepted

French-Seafood

❷❷

The walls of this brasserie are lined from floor to ceiling with tiny drawers which once

contained nuts and bolts, and there is a large metal staircase in the centre of the restaurant, hung with an enormous railway clock. The cooking is as delicious and unusual as the décor – lobster with sesame seeds and cider, ostrich steaks, and duck with oysters, as well as stunning shellfish.

LA TRUFFE NOIRE

La Table de l'Abbaye ⑧

R. de Belle Vue 12

∅ 646 3395

🚊 Trams 93 and 94

Open: Mon–Sat 1200–1430, 1900–2300, closed Sat lunch

Reservations essential

All credit cards accepted

French

€€€

Everything about this restaurant is refined: its location, just off avenue Louise in an elegant townhouse near the Abbey of Cambre; its dining room, with cream lace tablecloths, candles and huge floral displays; its garden terrace, dotted with classical statues, which seats 60; and its classic French menu and complementary wine list. Perfect for a romantic evening!

Tagawa ⑨

Av. Louise 271

∅ 640 5095

🚊 Bus 38 or trams 93 and 94

Open: Mon–Sat 1200–1400, 1900–2230, closed Sat lunch

Reservations recommended

All credit cards accepted

Japanese

€€€

The attention to detail in Brussels' top Japanese restaurant is exceptional, from the minimalist setting with its rice-paper partitions to the petite kimono-clad waitresses. Each dish is a work of art, tasting every bit as good as it looks. Choose from various set menus (*sashimi*, *tempura*, *shabu shabu*, *sukiyaki*), à la carte or, for a light meal, take a seat at the sushi counter.

La Truffe Noire ⑩

Blvd Cambre 12

∅ 640 4422

🚊 Trams 23, 90, 93 and 94

Open: Mon–Sat 1200–1400, 1900–2130

Reservations essential

All credit cards accepted

French-Italian

€€€

As its name suggests, the truffle participates in every dish of this world-class gastronomic restaurant at the edge of the Bois de la Cambre, and is best enjoyed on a business account! Chef Luigi Ciciriello has always been passionate about 'black diamonds'. He serves them sliced, grated, pickled, in pastry, with fish, meat, poultry and cheese.

▲ Brasseries Georges fish counter

IXELLES
Bars, cafés and pubs

L'Atelier ⑪

R. Elise 77

☎ 649 1953

🚍 Bus 71 or trams 93 and 94

Open: daily 1800–0300

No credit cards accepted

●

This popular watering-hole near the university attracts a varied crowd of students, chess players, and beer tourists, all keen to savour the two-hundred-plus beers on offer here. Some evenings there's live music too.

Atelier de la Truffe Noire ⑫

Av. Louise 300

☎ 640 5455

🚍 Bus 38 or trams 93 and 94

Open: Mon–Sat 0800–1800

All credit cards accepted

●●

If you can't afford dinner at **La Truffe Noire** (see page 71), console yourself with a light bite at this minimalist delicatessen-cum-café, owned by the grand eponymous restaurant. The menu features such delicacies as carpaccio, *foie gras* and a variety of truffle dishes at elevated but worthwhile prices.

Café Camille ⑬

Chaussée de Waterloo 559

☎ 345 9643

🚍 Bus 60

Open: Mon–Sat 1200–1430, 1900–2400, closed Sat lunch

No credit cards accepted

●●

It's unusual to see such a successful enterprise run by a brother-sister team, but in this relaxed and friendly bistro, off the beaten tourist track, it works a treat. One of the best features is the garden at the back with room for fifty covers in the cool shade of giant parasols. The food is modern French, the fish especially recommended, and the eclectic wine list reasonably priced.

Le Châtelein ⑭

Pl. du Châtelein 17

☎ 538 6794

🚍 Bus 54 or trams 81 and 82

Open: Mon–Sat 1030–2400

No credit cards accepted

●

A lively neighbourhood bar with a good selection of beers, sandwiches, grilled meats and local Bruxellois dishes, including *stoemp*, *carbonnade* and *waterzooi*, all enjoyed overlooking trendy place du Châtelein.

Chez Fleur ⑮

Chaussée de Boondael 326

☎ 640 0469

🚍 Bus 71 or trams 23, 90, 93 and 94

Open: daily 1200–1500, 1800–0030 (Sun 2400)

All credit cards accepted

●●

There is a host of trendy restaurants and bars near the university campuses and around Ixelles cemetery. Vietnamese cuisine has long been popular in Brussels and this small restaurant is one of the best in the area, in spite of its kitsch rococo décor.

En Face de Parachute ⑯

Chaussée de Waterloo 578

☎ 346 4741

🚍 Buses 38 and 60

Open: Tue–Sat 1200–1400, 1930–2300

No credit cards accepted

●●

This snug, navy-blue bistro was once a chemist's shop, and its original floor-to-ceiling wooden shelving now contains an impressive selection of wines. The seats are old tram seats, the food, cooked in a minute open kitchen in one corner of the restaurant, is basic but tasty, typically including such wholesome dishes as courgette vichyssoise, steak tartare, spinach ravioli and *stoemp*.

L112 ⑰

R. Lesbroussart 112

✆ 640 8343

🚊 Trams 81, 82, 93 and 94

Open: Mon–Sat 1200–1430, 1900–2230, closed Sat lunch and Mon evening

Reservations recommended

All credit cards accepted

❶❶

A typically Ixellois restaurant with a cool, understated dining room in warm, earthy tones, a sunny walled garden with a handful of tables, and a small but imaginative menu based on fresh seasonal produce. Try the toasted goats' cheese with *sirop de Liège*, then ostrich steak with prune sauce, followed by a mascarpone mousse flavoured with orange blossom.

Le Macaron ⑱

R. du Mail 1

✆ 537 8943

🚌 Buses 54 and 60 or trams 81 and 82

Open: Tue–Sun 1200–1430, 1830–2200, closed Sat lunch and Sun lunch

No credit cards accepted

❶

Come here for hearty portions of pasta in fun surroundings. The restaurant is decorated like an old-fashioned corner store, with ancient weighing scales on the counter, old metal advertising signs

on the walls and shelves stocked with ancient jars, packets and tins of household essentials. The walls are of bare brick, the tables wooden and rough, and the clientele lively and young.

Raconte-Moi des Salades ⑲

Pl. du Châtelein 19

✆ 534 2727

🚌 Bus 54 or trams 81 and 82

Open: Mon–Sat 1200–1430, 1900–2300

❶❶

Located right beside the place du Châtelein fruit and vegetable market, this jam-packed café serves over thirty different types of fresh, crisp salads ranging from beef, rosemary, rocket and parmesan to the five vegetable 'végétarienne' special. The name

'Raconte-Moi des Salades' is a play on words, meaning 'Don't talk nonsense!'.

Thoumieux ⑳

R. Américaine 124

✆ 538 9909

🚌 Buses 38 and 60 or trams 93 and 94

Open: daily 1200–1430, 1900–2330, closed Sun evening

Reservations recommended

American Express

❶❶

Among the most famous brasseries of Paris, Thoumieux can now be enjoyed in Brussels. Its versatile menu specialises in dishes from southwestern France and there is also an extremely popular seafood bar on the pavement outside, where you can while away the evening sipping champagne and downing oysters.

▲ Le Macaron

IXELLES
Shops, markets and picnic sites

Shops

Les Caprices du Bailli ㉑

R. du Bailli 75

🚊 Bus 54 or trams 81 and 82

Open: Tue–Sat 0800–1800, Sun 0800–1400

No credit cards accepted

The tempting gateaux displayed in the window entice passers-by into this authentic art-nouveau patisserie store to try the delicious fruit tarts, florentines, cherry *clafouti* and speciality *friands* (tiny orange blossom-flavoured cupcakes).

Capucine ㉒

R. Simonis 62

🚊 Bus 54 or trams 81 and 82

Open: Mon–Sat 1100–1900 (Wed 1930)

💳 💳 💳

The exciting range of stylish and exotic products, displayed on illuminated shelving in this ultra-modern delicatessen, are definitely aimed at gourmets. There's a minimalist dining room at the back serving a small selection of aromatic dishes influenced by the flavours of Italy, Provence, Morocco and India.

Le Chai de Marianne ㉓

R. du Page 58

🚊 Buses 54 and 60 or trams 81 and 82

Open: Tue–Fri 1030–1900, Sat 1400–1930

No credit cards accepted

Fine wines mingle with fine art in this small, back-street wine shop, specialising in Burgundy, the Loire and Champagne regions of France, together with a choice selection of bottles from Italy, Spain and the New World. Visit on a Saturday to join in the weekly *dégustations* (1400–1900), whilst admiring the monthly changing exhibitions of work by local artists and photographers which adorn the walls.

Le Déjeuner sur l'Herbe ㉔

Av. Louis Lepoutre 6

🚊 Bus 60

Open: Tue–Sun 1100–2000

No credit cards accepted

As the name suggests, this old-fashioned delicatessen, contained in an original *fin-de-siècle* pharmacy store, contains everything imaginable for 'lunch on the grass', together with the most comprehensive selection of homemade soups and ready-made dishes in Belgium.

La Framboisier Doré ㉕

R. du Bailli 35

🚊 Bus 54 or trams 81 and 82

Open: Tue–Fri 1130–2300, Sat–Sun 1230–2300

No credit cards accepted

This charming *glacier* still makes ice cream the old-fashioned way without artificial colouring, flavouring or additives. Their best sellers are vanilla, chocolate and *speculoos* (caramelised biscuit), but those with more adventurous palates will enjoy *sirop*

▲ Le Déjeuner sur l'Herbe

de Liège, Kriek beer, gooseberry, lavender, rose and jasmine.

Gourmand Gaillard

Chaussée de Vleurgat 192

🚊 Buses 38 and 60 or trams 93 and 94

Open: Mon–Sat 0800–1900

No credit cards accepted

This up-market cakeshop-cum-café is a popular luncheon spot for smart Ixellois ladies who come clutching their designer shopping bags. It sells both sweet and savoury tarts, sandwiches, gateaux, chocolates and patisseries to take away or eat in the minimalist dining area.

Maison Felix ㉗

R. Washington 14

🚊 Buses 38 and 60

Open: delicatessen: Tue–Sat 1000–2030, Sun 1000–1300; restaurant: Tue–Sat 1200–1430, 1900–2130

All credit cards accepted

The place to purchase luxury picnic fare from this chic, modern delicatessen alongside Park Tenbosch – smoked salmon, terrines, cold cuts, cheeses, fruits, vegetables and wines – and be sure to return later for an ice cream from the famous Parisian producer, Berthillon.

Le Palais du Gourmet ㉘

R. du Bailli 106

🚊 Bus 54 or trams 81 and 82

Open: Tue–Sat 0900–1930

Well-to-do shoppers of Ixelles come to this exclusive delicatessen for their champagnes, wines, cheeses and caviar. There are also cold cuts, *antipasti*, mustards, oils and preserves, an impressive choice of spirits and liqueurs, and the occasional wine-tasting on Saturday afternoons (*1300–1900*).

La Septième Tasse ㉙

R. du Bailli 37

🚊 Bus 54 or trams 81 and 82

Open: Tue–Sat 1100–1900

No credit cards accepted

This highly specialised shop is a must for tea-drinkers, with over a hundred different varieties from around the world to see, smell and taste, together with an elegant selection of teapots and tea-making accessories.

Markets

Place du Châtelein ㉚

🚊 Bus 54 or trams 81 and 82

Open: Wed 1400–1900

This colourful and fragrant market has an almost village feel with its clutter of specialist stalls selling farm-produced goats' cheese, wild mushrooms, olives, fruit, vegetables and fresh herbs. An ideal

place to assemble a picnic, or to tuck into the various hot quiches, tortilla, kebabs and crêpes from the assortment of takeaway stands.

Picnic sites

Bois de la Cambre ㉛

Main entrance on av. Louise

🚊 Bus 38, 41 and 60 or trams 23, 90, 93 and 94

Formerly part of the ancient Forest of Soignes, this magnificent landscaped park is the green lung of Brussels, with extensive woodlands, a boating lake and plenty of grassy areas ideal for picnics and ball games. It is especially popular on Sundays when transport is banned and the park rediscovers its natural calm and, in summer months, outdoor concerts are staged among the trees.

Park Tenbosch ㉜

Between Chaussée de Vleurgat, r. Hector Denis and r. des Mélèzes

🚊 Buses 38 and 60 or trams 93 and 94

Despite its small size, this arboretum is one of the city's most pleasant parks, with its age-old beeches, hazels, pines and poplars and over fifty rare species of tree. There's a play area for children with swings and climbing frames, a couple of small ponds, a tennis court and a terrace for *boules*.

Café society

A sense of cosiness

Café culture is *de rigueur* in Brussels. There's one on virtually every street corner and, although they all serve coffee, soft drinks, *genevers* (Belgian gin), wines, and food, Belgian cafés mostly serve beers – and sometimes there's such an impressive choice that they even have a separate 'beer menu'. This excellence of Belgian food and drink belongs to a long tradition of sociability. Right back in the days of Pieter Breughel the Elder, social life revolved around the *kroeg*, the bar in the local inn. His paintings bear testimony to such joyful gatherings, and little has changed. Still today, people from all walks of life – whether students, gays, shoppers, Eurocrats or OAPs – all frequent cafés, to linger over an espresso and a slice of cake, to sip a cocktail, to drink beer, or to enjoy a meal, and everyone enjoys the convivial atmosphere.

Belgians make little or no distinction between the names café, bar, brasserie, pub or *estaminet* (tavern). Whatever you call them, you'll be amazed by the sheer variety of drinking establishments: stylish art-nouveau brasseries, age-old, weather-beaten, smoke-stained locales, chic minimalist designer cafés, hi-tech cyber bars, elegant Champs Elysées-style cafés, Irish bars serving Guinness, and exotic cocktail bars. But they all have one common factor – a sense of *gezelligheid* or cosiness, a quality highly cherished by the Belgians. As opening hours are not officially restricted, bars and cafés can stay open as long as they want. Most close around 0200, although at weekends some remain open much later.

One of the most sophisticated areas for café-hopping is Le Sablon. Grand-Place has a varied selection of up-market bars too, although you pay above the odds for the privilege of drinking in the main square (but not necessarily in the streets surrounding it). The university zone of Ixelles (near the cemetery) has long been a popular, upbeat venue for the trendy youth of Brussels to drink beers and flavoured vodkas late into the night, and recently place Saint-Géry, near the Bourse, has also become a favoured café nightspot. Further afield, the EU district is the area to go for Irish and English-style pubs, while

▲ La Porteuse d'Eau

Saint-Gilles offers a broad choice of bars and cafés remarkably untouched by tourism.

With Brussels as the world capital of art nouveau, it's hardly surprising that some of its finest cafés are in this pure *fin-de-siècle* style, including **Le Falstaff** (*see page 23*), **Le Perroquet** (*see page 44*) and **La Porteuse d'Eau** (*see page 84*). Perhaps most renowned is **La Morte Subite** (*r. Montagne-aux-Herbes-Potagères 7; ℘ 513 1318; open: Mon–Sat 1030–0100, Sun 1230–0100*), once a favourite haunt of the great Bruxellois singer, Jacques Brel. Everything here is original – the counter, the mirrors, the seating, the stained glass, even the radiators – and the walls are stained from generations of smokers. La Morte Subite is definitely *the* place to try Kriek, Faro and Gueuze, as they brew it themselves. The name, which means 'Sudden Death', does not refer to the effect of drink upon the patrons but to a dice game that was once popular in this café.

Another unusual name, and another legendary *estaminet*, housed in a dark 17th-century building, is **La Fleur en Papier Doré**, 'The Flower in Gilded Paper' (*r. des Alexiens 55; ℘ 511 1659; open: 1130–0100 (Fri–Sat 0300)*), where René Magritte was a patron, and Max Ernst held art exhibitions. Throughout the 1920s it was the locale of the Belgian surrealists and Dadaists, and the walls are still covered with their pictures, writings and graffiti.

Café Metropole (*see page 22*) is one of the city's grandest cafés – a riot of curvaceous *fin-de-siècle* wood, leather, stained glass, mirrors, and chandeliers – and a great venue to enjoy the local aperitif *'half en half'* (half champagne, half white wine) on the terrace. Equally celebrated, **De Ultieme Hallucinatie** (*r. Royale 316; ℘ 217 0614; open: 1100–0200*) boasts an equally impressive interior of authentic art-nouveau wood, glass and pale green ironwork. The restaurant section is quite pricey, but the adjoining café with its plain wooden chairs and tables, its lengthy beer list, and its daily parade of Brussels' characters, makes it the perfect backdrop for a leisurely liquid break.

> **With Brussels as the world capital of art nouveau, it's hardly surprising that some of its finest cafés are in this pure *fin-de-siècle* style.**

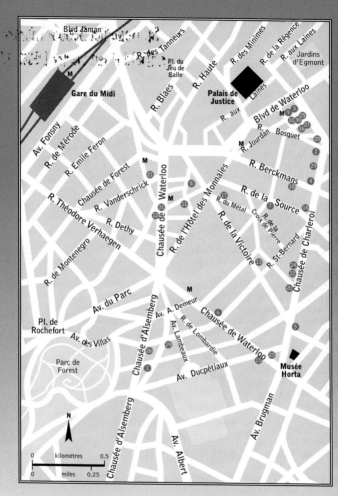

Saint-Gilles

The charming residential commune of Saint-Gilles is one of Brussels' most atmospheric districts, with its endearing little squares, its elegant art-nouveau houses and a host of characterful shops, cafés and bistros. The area is especially popular in fine weather, as most of the bars have pavement terraces, and many of the restaurants boast secluded gardens.

Aux Anges ❶

R. A. Diderich 33–37

☎ 539 3906

🚊 Trams 23, 55 and 90 or bus 54

Open: Mon–Sat 1900–2300

Reservations recommended

[VISA]

Italian

💶💶

Stepping inside this place is rather like walking into heaven! The décor is completely over-the-top, based entirely on a theme of angels, with cherub frescos smothering the walls and ceilings, floating about on white fluffy clouds. Modish young lovers dine by candlelight in intimate alcoves, seduced by the setting and the aromatic cuisine. Typical dishes include aubergine roulade, penne with *foie gras* and wild mushrooms with truffle oil.

ATM (à toi Mauricette) ❷

Chaussée de Charleroi 29

☎ 534 7018

🚊 Trams 91 and 92

Open: Mon–Sat 1200–1500, 1900–2300, closed Sat lunch

Reservations recommended

All credit cards accepted

French-Italian

💶💶

Lively yet cool, this 'in' restaurant just off avenue Louise draws a chic, sleek crowd to its minimalist interior. Dining is on two levels or in the equally designer terrace-garden. The ultra-modern ambience is a little clinical, but the warm service more than compensates, as does the menu – a trendy choice of salads and seasonal dishes, imaginatively prepared by brilliant young chef, Mauricette.

Les Capucines ❸

R. Jourdan 22

☎ 538 6924

🚇 Metro Louise

Open: Mon–Sat 1200–1430, 1900–2230, closed Mon lunch

Reservations recommended

All credit cards accepted

French

💶💶💶

Chef Pierre Burtomboy continues to surprise his clients with his top-notch, highly personal cuisine: the imaginative menu says it all … fresh pea vichyssoise, aubergine caviar, suckling pig roasted with *harissa*, lamb cutlets with nuts, thyme and lemon, and frozen peach and raspberry soup with green tea and fresh mint.

Ma Folle de Soeur ❹

Chaussée de Charleroi 53

☎ 538 2239

🚊 Trams 91 and 92

Open: Mon–Sat 1200–1415, 1900–2230

Reservations recommended

All credit cards accepted

French

💶💶

Just a stone's throw from bustling place Stéphanie, this homely bistro is popular for a quick lunch or for a more relaxed dinner in the evening, with its appetising home cooking, its regularly changing menu, its wine list at thirst-quenching prices, and its cosy country-kitchen surroundings. In summer months there's a delightful garden with 25 covers. The raw salmon marinated with fresh herbs, the kidneys in mustard and the roast cod are especially recommended.

Le Forcado ❺

Chaussée de Charleroi 192

☎ 537 9220

🚊 Trams 91 and 92

Open: Tue–Sat 1200–1400, 1900–2200

Reservations recommended

All credit cards accepted

Portuguese

💶💶💶

For over fifteen years chef Joaquim Braz de Loiveira has proudly presented the gastronomic traditions of his home country to the Bruxellois. Start with the *mosaique du Portugal*, then try one of a choice of paella, seafood risotto, various cod dishes, lamb ragout or peppered port with shellfish. For dessert, the artisan patisseries from **Le Petit Forcado** (the adjoining delicatessen situated on the corner of rue Américaine) are always a special treat.

Grandeur Nature

Chaussée de Waterloo 296

Ø 544 1823

Trams 91 and 92

Open: Mon–Fri 1200–1430, 1900–2300, Sat–Sun 1900–2300

French-Vegetarian

Reservations recommended

€€

It's impossible to miss this jolly corner restaurant with its dazzling tangerine-coloured façade. The monthly changing menu contains a healthy choice of market-fresh dishes (roast tuna with bacon and balsamic vinegar, veal escalope with sage and rosemary), with more vegetarian choices than usual (spinach roulade, quorn casserole with nuts and ginger), and some amazing desserts. Don't miss the peach *tarte Tatin* (upside-down caramelised peach sponge pudding)!

Inada 7

R. de la Source 73

✆ 538 0113

🚊 Trams 91 and 92

Open: Tue–Sat 1200–1400, 1900–2300, closed Sat lunch

Reservations recommended

All credit cards accepted

French

€€€

The menu here is essentially French, but with Asian subtleties. It includes such delicacies as liver mousse with a port sauce, and cod grilled with seaweed, cream and fine herbs, served with a stunning list of wines from around the world and the largest choice of port in Belgium. Everything is served with exquisite attention to detail and perfect discretion.

Aux Mille et Une Nuits 8

R. du Moscou 5

✆ 537 4127

🚊 Trams 23, 55 and 90 or bus 48

Open: daily 1800–2330

Reservations recommended at weekends

 American Express

Tunisian

€€

Just off the main square of Saint-Gilles, this atmospheric Tunisian restaurant attracts an eclectic crowd, united by their appreciation of tasty, well-priced North African cuisine. With its midnight blue, star-clad walls, its brocades and richly coloured wall rugs, traditional lamps, ceramics and music, the small but exotic interior is full of eastern promise, which the food delivers. The *salade mechouin* (tomatoes, olives and onions with *harissa*) is spicy, the couscous hearty and filling, and the *tagines* both fragrant and delicious.

Al Piccolo Mondo 9

R. Jourdan 19

✆ 538 8794

🚊 Metro Louise

Open: daily 1200–1500, 1800–0100

Reservations recommended

All credit cards accepted

Italian

€€

At Piccolo Mondo (Small World) think more 'mondo' than 'piccolo', as this sizeable trattoria in popular rue Jourdan is always jam-packed. The interior is nothing special, but the service is stylish and the food is always delicious and reliable. The menu includes such classics as seafood spaghetti and Venetian-style veal (with onions and gravy) as well as carpaccio of scallops, linguine with lobster, and other more innovative dishes.

Riverside Café 10

R. Jourdan 24

✆ 534 0999

🚊 Metro Louise

Open: Tue–Sun 1000–2400

Reservations unnecessary

All credit cards accepted

Belgian

€€

This unpretentious modern establishment – more of a restaurant than a café – serves a varied menu of Belgian cuisine. Specialities include shrimp croquettes, vegetable cake with tomato and fresh parsley sauce, ray with caper butter and chicken *waterzooi*. Choose a table on the sunny terrace – it's a superb location for people-watching!

SAINT-GILLES
Bars, cafés and pubs

Brasserie de l'Union [11]

Parvis de St-Gilles 55

☏ 538 1579

🚋 Trams 23, 55 and 90 or bus 48

Open: daily 0800–0100

No credit cards

€

This traditional venue, with its zinc bar and small tables tightly packed by the windows, overlooking the daily fruit and vegetable market, is always lively. At lunchtimes the *plat du jour* is superb value, and occasionally there's live music at weekends.

Brasserie Verschueren [12]

Parvis de St-Gilles 11–13

☏ 539 4068

🚋 Trams 23, 55 and 90 or bus 48

Open: Tue–Sun 0800–0100 (Fri–Sat 0200)

No credit cards

€

A simple, weather-beaten locals' bar, centrally located on Saint-Gilles' main square and appealing to all ages, with its scruffy wooden tables and benches, newspapers on scrolls, the local football divisions posted up on the wall and, unusually for Brussels, a no-smoking area. There is a small selection of snacks (portions of cheese, olives, salami, and so on) and a fair choice of beers including their own potent 7 per cent brew, *la bière Verschueren*.

Café Cartigny [13]

R. de la Victoire 158

☏ 538 7524

🚋 Trams 81, 82, 91 and 92

Open: Wed–Sun 1700–2230

💳 💳

€

This simple, spacious café-theatre with cool, icy-green décor, modern paintings by local artists and marble-topped tables, serves a limited but nutritious daily menu of homemade soups, pâtés, meat and fish dishes, some good vegetarian choices, and dazzling desserts. Some evenings there are poetry readings or other amateur-dramatic productions.

Chelsea [14]

Chaussée de Charleroi 85

☏ 544 1977

🚋 Trams 91 and 92

Open: Mon–Sat 1200–1400, 1900–2300 (Fri–Sat 2400), closed Sat lunch and Mon evening

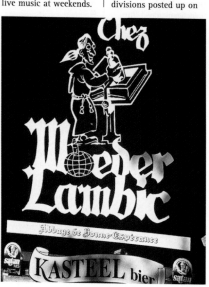

All credit cards accepted

€€€

This sophisticated wine bar and restaurant blends comfort and tradition with modernity, in its décor, service and cuisine. The bar offers 40 wines by the glass, and the restaurant presents an irresistible French menu including scallops with *foie gras* glazed in balsamic vinegar, and roasted sea devil with a tomato and basil coulis. Reserve a table in advance if you want to eat outside.

La Cigale 🕦

Chaussée de Waterloo 329

☎ 538 1721

🚊 Trams 81 and 82

Open: Tue–Sun 0900–0100

All credit cards accepted

€

Always jam-packed with locals, this family-run bar has a rustic pub-like atmosphere with its dark, comfortable interior and walls decorated with beer adverts. The small restaurant section serves wholesome traditional cuisine of sausage and *stoemp*, black pudding, ham on the bone and mussels in season. There are several tables outside on the pavement to watch the Saint-Gilleois go by.

La Crémerie de la Vache 🕦

R. Jean Stas 6

☎ 538 2818

🚇 Metro Louise

Open: daily 0800–1900

▲ Moeder Lambic

No credit cards accepted

€

Soothingly decorated from top to toe in cream, this stylish café-cum-tearoom serves a tasty menu of tarts, cakes, quiches, salads, fruit juices and milkshakes to health-conscious shoppers. Try their organic bread, their patisseries and their ice creams – the vanilla with honey and lavender is especially moreish.

Kim's Pub 🕥

R. du Métal 4

☎ 538 9157

🚇 Metro Hôtel des Monnaies

Open: Sun–Fri 1100–1430, 1900–2300

€€

Kim, the friendly Lebanese owner, ensures a warm welcome to his pint-sized bar with its brick-clad interior, dark wooden beams and tiny cramped tables. There's even a sunny pavement terrace, where you can tuck into a variety of salads, lasagne, fondues,

do-it-yourself *pierrade* (where you cook your own meat on a hot stone slab) and Lebanese dishes.

À Malte 🕦

R. Berckmans 30

☎ 537 0991

🚊 Trams 91 and 92

Open: Sun–Fri 1000–2400, Sat 1600–2400

€

This eccentric venue is all things to all people – a café, restaurant, bar and tea salon all under one roof. Crammed full of bric-à-brac, deep leather settees, ancient portraits, pot plants and sculptures, it has a homely feel, and is especially popular for a relaxing candlelit drink in the pretty walled garden by night.

Moeder Lambic 🕦

R. de Savoie 68

☎ 539 1419

🚊 Trams 81 and 82

Open: daily 1600–0230

No credit cards accepted

€

As Lambic is one of the main types of Belgian

beer, it seems appropriate that a bar named *Moeder Lambic* (meaning 'Mother Lambic') should stock over 1000 different beers. Considering the length of the beer list, the bar itself is small but, due to its hidden location well away from the tourist beat, it rarely gets overcrowded. Try one of the *bières de collection* ('collectors' beers' – no longer in production) or a beer cocktail: the 'Three Musketeers', for instance, contains Duvel, Hoegaarden and Kriek beers with orange juice!

Perbacco 20

Chaussée de Charleroi 197

☏ 537 6799

🚋 Trams 91 and 92

Open: Mon–Sat 1200–1400, 1900–2200 (Fri–Sat 2300), closed Sat lunch

🅿🅿

This small, minimalist restaurant is understated without being bland – as is the food (fussy, simple Italian cooking), the décor (a warm blend of terracotta, cream and turquoise), and the clientele (trendy but appreciative of refined cuisine). The adjoining shop sells fine wines, oils and takeaway pasta dishes.

La Porteuse d'Eau 21

Av. Jean Volders 48

☏ 537 6646

🚋 Trams 23, 55 and 90 or bus 48

Open: daily 1000–2400; kitchen open 1200–1500, 1800–2300

No credit cards

🅿🅿

With its curvaceous stained glass, its light, airy wood-and-mirrored interior and its central spiral staircase, this stylish brasserie is a must for fans of art nouveau, popular with the bourgeoisie of Saint-Gilles for coffee or a full meal served by helpful waiters in long white aprons. The three-course lunch is especially good value.

Les Salons de l'Atalaide 22

Chaussée de Charleroi 89

☏ 537 2154

🚋 Trams 91 and 92

Open: daily 1130–1500, 1900–2330

All credit cards accepted

🅿🅿

This is rather like dining in a chocolate box, with its sumptuous surroundings and kitsch décor. Start off with a drink in the exotic North African-style upstairs bar, before progressing downstairs into the vast main dining room – a converted auction hall, bedecked with lavish drapes, chandeliers, shell-encrusted mirrors, marble statuary, flying carpets and candles in bottles. The food doesn't quite match up to the surroundings but it nonetheless remains one of the most popular eateries in town,

attracting a chic crowd. Booking is essential.

Tea for Two 23

Chaussée de Waterloo 394

☏ 538 3896

🚋 Trams 81 and 82

Open: Tue–Sun 1100–1900

💳 💳

🅿

'Boire du thé, c'est oublier un instant le bruit du monde...' ('to drink tea is to forget, for a moment, the noise of the world') is written on the door of this English-style teashop. When you're sitting in the shade of the tiny walled garden or in the sanctuary of one of the small, quaint backrooms, sipping tea scented with lotus flowers, mandarin essence or rose petals from a fine porcelain teacup, you will see what they mean!

Le Temps Delire 24

Chaussée de Charleroi 175–7

☏ 538 1210

🚋 Trams 91 and 92

Open: Mon–Fri 1200–1430, Mon–Thu 1900–2230, Fri–Sat 1900–2330

All credit cards accepted

🅿🅿

A popular, fashionable bistro on three levels, decorated in dark wood, bare brick and modern lighting, and providing a cosy, intimate atmosphere in which to enjoy an appealing choice of salads, fresh pastas, meat and fish dishes. In summer there is also al fresco dining.

SAINT-GILLES
Shops, markets and picnic sites

Shops

Caviar House 25

R. Jean Stas 19a

Ⓜ Metro Louise

Open: Mon–Sat 1000–1900

All credit cards accepted

You'll find all the fine things in life here ... six different types of caviar, Scotch whiskies, Russian vodkas, French wines, teas, jams, smoked salmon, *foie gras* and even hundred-year-old champagne.

Champignac 26

Chaussée d'Alsemberg 108

Ⓜ Bus 48

Open: Tue–Sat 1000–1900

No credit cards accepted

This newly opened shop sells wild mushrooms of every shape size and colour, along with everything associated with them – mushroom books, pasta filled with mushroom, sausages containing mushrooms and a handful of choice accompaniments.

Dille & Kamille 27

R. Jean Stas

Ⓜ Metro Louise

Open: daily 0930–1830

The emphasis here is on natural products. From the fragrant pots of

fresh herbs in the entrance, to the stacks of crockery, the gleaming racks of knives, the colourful paper napkins and the neat rows of mustards, jams, oils and vinegars, there's everything here that you could ever need for your country-style kitchen.

Godiva 28

Chaussée de Charleroi 11

Ⓜ Trams 91, 92, 93 and 94

Open: Mon–Sat 0930–1830, Sun 1100–1900

All credit cards accepted

The most famous of all Belgian chocolate manufacturers, with shops all round the globe.

Mig's Wine World 29

Chaussée de Charleroi 43

Ⓜ Trams 91 and 92

Open: Tue–Sat 1000–1800

All credit cards accepted

This large, fashionable wine merchant specialises in bottles from the New World, notably New Zealand, Australia, Chile and South Africa.

Traiteur Coppé 30

R. Jean Stas 13

Ⓜ Metro Louise

Open: Mon–Sat 1000–1900

All credit cards accepted

A small but select grocer's, selling fine wines,

coffees, teas and preserves, and Dandoy biscuits (*see page 24*). The deli counter has a mouth-watering choice of cold cuts, salamis, pâtés, cheeses and *antipasti* – ideal for a picnic (with bread from **La Crémerie de la Vache** opposite – *see page 83*).

Markets

Parvis de Saint-Gilles 31

Parvis de St-Gilles/r. du Fort

Ⓜ Trams 23, 55 and 90 or bus 48

Open: Tue–Sun 0600–1230

Join the Saint-Gilleois in their daily purchase of fruit and vegetables from this lively, local market.

▲ Champignac

An incurably sweet tooth

The butter eaters

Belgian cakes, tarts, biscuits and desserts, many still made according to ancient country recipes, are one of the most beloved aspects of the local cuisine. In Brussels, in particular, there is a bewildering choice of bakeries, pastry shops, sweet shops, waffle-houses and teashops in which to indulge the national sweet tooth. Bruxellois have long been known for their partiality to sweet things. Even François I's doctor referred to them as *bouffers de beurre* ('the butter eaters'). And can you blame them? The tantalising window displays of tarts overflowing with summer fruits; dense, nutty fruitcakes; lacy, butter cookies; fluffy cheesecakes and gooey chocolate extravaganzas are undeniably hard to resist.

Cakes and pastries are an inseparable part of city life, from the afternoon ritual of sitting in a café or tea salon with pot of freshly brewed coffee and an array of glistening fruit tarts, to the Sunday morning visit to the

▲ Le Pain Quotidien

local bakery for an assortment of freshly baked *koeken* for the breakfast table. *Koeken* (pastries) come in various shapes and sizes – *boterkoeken, suikerkoeken, peperkoeken* … all made with a sweet buttery dough, loaded with pearl sugar, currants, dried fruit and nuts or simply flavoured with vanilla, cinnamon and allspice.

Bread too is a basic part of every meal. As the old country saying goes: 'as long as there's bread on the table, there's hope'. Most bakers, including **Le Pain Quotidien** (*see pages 43 and 54*), offer a daily baked assortment of whole-wheat, white, rye, sour-dough, raisin and various spiced fruit loaves to choose from, and many are eaten sliced with a generous layer of homemade jam, chocolate spread or *sirop de Liège* (a quince and apple spread). *Koekebrood* (a rich, brioche-type bread with raisins) is especially delicious. They say of someone who is kind and generous that 'they have a heart of *koekebrood*'. Another traditional bread is *pain à la grecque* (from the Flemish *brood van der gracht*, meaning 'bread from the ditch') – a heavy fruit loaf, originally distributed to the poor and needy in rue du Fossé-aux-Loups in medieval times.

Belgian **biscuits** are almost as famous as their chocolates and, in particular, the biscuits produced by **Dandoy** (*see page 24*) in the aptly named rue au Beurre near Grand-Place. Try their *speculoos* – thin, crisp, buttery biscuits made with cinnamon, ginger, nutmeg and cloves, which at Christmas come in the shape of St Nicolas. Every café in Brussels serves a *speculoos* biscuit with each cup of coffee. Another classic is wafer-thin almond biscuits. Shaped in rectangles and beautifully packaged in ornamental tins, they make wonderful presents.

Confections made with almonds have long been popular in Belgium: try **Dandoy** for marzipan, **Les Caprices du Bailli** (*see page 74*) for frangipan (tiny marzipan-based cakes) and **Dragées Marechal** (*see page 15*) for *dragées*, whole almonds covered in a hard casing of pastel-coloured sugar, traditionally given as gifts to celebrate a baby's birth.

For the most refined and creative cakes in town, **Wittamer** (*see page 44*), established in 1910, is something of an institution. Here *pâtisserie* has been raised to an art form. Each tart, cake and pastry is meticulously handcrafted by Wittamer family artisans, then best savoured with a Belgian-style cappuccino (sprinkled with shavings of Wittamer chocolate) on the sunny pavement terrace outside.

At the other end of the scale, those with a sweet tooth and into

▲ Wittamer

> **Each tart, cake and pastry is meticulously handcrafted by Wittamer family artisans, then best savoured with a Belgian-style cappuccino.**

'fast food' can sink their teeth into luscious, freshly cooked, feather-light *gaufres* (waffles) from one of the many **waffle** stands dotted throughout the city. Just follow your nose until you find one, wafting delicious smells of baking waffles and caramelised sugar into the street. During the last decade, sugar waffles (*gaufres liégeoises*), chocolate-coated waffles and plain Brussels waffles (*gaufres de Bruxelles*) served with whipped cream, jam and sometimes fresh fruit, have become one of the most popular street foods in Belgium. Recommended stands include **Belgaufra** (*chaussée d'Ixelles 19*) in Louise, and **Vigafure** (*blvd Anspach 40*), **Belgaufra** (*r. Tabora 6*) and **Au Gâteau de Bruxelles** (*r. Marché aux Herbes 113*) in the city centre.

Food etiquette and culture

'So prodigiously good was the eating and drinking on board these sluggish but most comfortable vessels, that there are legends extant of an English traveller who, coming to Belgium for a week, and travelling in one of these boats, was so delighted with the fare there that he went backwards and forwards from Ghent to Bruges perpetually until the railroads were invented, when he drowned himself on the last trip of the passage-boat.' (From *Vanity Fair* by William Makepeace Thackeray, 1847–8.)

It is an increasingly well-known fact that Belgian cuisine ranks among the best in Europe, with more Michelin-rated restaurants per head than France. Eating out is a Bruxellois passion. However, with over 1 800 venues to choose from, Michelin's gastronomic temples are far from being the normal place to eat out in Brussels. Most people frequent the many bistros, French-style brasseries, cafés, old-fashioned *estaminets* (taverns) and bars – usually small, cosy establishments, frequently combining restaurant and bar, thereby providing a relaxed and flexible approach, typical of the authentic Belgian dining experience. Eating and drinking are both of equal importance in Brussels. The Belgians are the world's biggest beer drinkers, after all, and in some places you may find that the beer list is longer than the menu.

WHERE TO EAT

Little distinction is made between the various types of Bruxellois eatery. As a general rule, the brasseries tend to be larger than the bistros, both are slightly more formal than the cafés and bars, and they usually have a more comprehensive menu. In a bar or a café, customers can order anything from a coffee, a beer and a snack to a full-blown meal, although some smaller bars only serve *petite restauration* (sandwiches and light snacks). In a brasserie or bistro it is more common to eat than to just drink, while *estaminets* are first-and-foremost watering-holes frequented by locals, although some serve wholesome, traditional food as well. The atmosphere varies from place to place according to the décor – from chic, ultra-modern, 'designer' bars to welcoming, country-kitchen style cafés; and from snug little bistros with bare-brick walls crammed with antique clutter, to elegant art-nouveau brasseries, so perfectly restored they could almost be museum pieces.

WHAT TO EAT

Apart from native Belgian fare, Brussels is also one of the best

European cities for sampling a wide range of international cuisine – French predominates (most of the classier restaurants in town serve French menus), but you will also find Caribbean, Greek, Indian, Italian, Japanese, Mexican, Russian, Spanish, Thai, Turkish and Vietnamese. The Belgians are also among Europe's biggest fish eaters. You can enjoy the freshest of seafood platters in the city's many first-rate fish restaurants, especially those in the streets around place Sainte-Catherine.

WHEN TO EAT

Opening hours vary from one establishment to another. Brasseries, bistros, *estaminets* and cafés generally keep bar hours: some open seven days a week as early as 0700, serve non-stop cuisine from around 1100 to midnight, and eventually close in the small hours. More formal restaurants typically open from 1200 to 1430 and from 1800 to 2230 or 2300. Many close on Saturday lunchtimes and Sundays or Mondays, and some shut down altogether in July and August.

Always phone in advance to check the opening times to avoid disappointment and, for more up-market establishments, it is advisable to make a reservation.

PRICES

Eating out in Brussels is not cheap, but there are establishments to suit all tastes and pockets, from the most refined of gourmet temples to the humble *friterie* (chip stands) on street corners. Standards are invariably high, and even the touristic haunts serve reasonable, and often top-quality food. Most of the tourist-oriented restaurants are centred around Grand-Place – an area with such a glut of restaurants that is it sometimes described as 'the stomach of Brussels'. Lunch menus are considerably less expensive than evening ones, and the *plat du jour* (a main course 'meal of the day') is often a bargain – in most places it's served all day. A service charge is automatically included on the bill, but it is nevertheless customary to leave a tip of around 5–10 per cent depending on service.

Menu decoder

Although Belgium is a bilingual country (with French and Flemish as its official languages), French predominates in Brussels and most menus are written in French. Here is a selection of the most typical Bruxellois dishes, together with some of the more commonly found regional dishes:

andouilles/andouillettes – rich sausages made of offal

anguilles au vert – the local preparation for eels, in a green fresh herb sauce

asperge flamande – warm asparagus with butter and chopped eggs

ballekes – meatballs of minced beef cooked in tomato sauce

bière d'abbaye – 'abbey' beers are made at monasteries which are not of the Trappist order

bière blanche – a light, refreshing, 'white beer' (also called *witbier*), made of wheat and with a distinctive, cloudy appearance, caused by the yeast mixing with the beer. It is often drunk with a slice of lemon

bière trappiste – a rich, dark 'Trappist' beer, produced under the supervision of monks at Chimay, Orval, Rochefort, Westmalle and Westvleteren, which also comes as a *double* with 6–7 per cent alcohol or a *tripel* at 8–9 per cent

bloedpans au vinaigre de xérès – a large black pudding with sherry vinegar

boudin blanc – liver sausage

boudin noir – blood sausage

café liégeois – coffee ice cream with whipped cream

canard à la bière cassis – duck with blackcurrant beer sauce

carbonnade flamande – beef braised with beer and onions, and sometimes carrots and prunes

charcuterie – cold cuts

chicon – chicory (also known as *witloof*)

choesels – offal cooked in red wine or beer

choucroute – sauerkraut

couque – a butter croissant, either plain or with raisins

cramique – a type of sugary bun or loaf containing raisins

crêpe flamande – pancake with caramelised apples and prunes

crevettes roses/grises – red/grey shrimps – often used in salads or croquettes

croque monsieur – cheese and ham on toast

croquettes de crevettes grises – shrimp croquettes

croquettes de fromage – cheese croquettes

coquilles oostendaise – scallops in a cream sauce

dame blanche – vanilla ice cream with melted chocolate

escargots Ixelles – snail and mushroom tartlets

faisan à la Brabançonne – pheasant in butter, white wine and chicory

Faro – 'Lambic' beer (*see below*) but with the addition of brown sugar

flamiche – a vegetable and cream tart

foie de veau à la Rodenbach – calves' liver with Rodenbach red ale

framboise – raspberry-flavoured beer

frites – chips

friterie – a chip stand

gaufres au chocolat – chocolate waffles

genever – gin

Gueuze – a naturally sour beer made by blending old 'Lambic' with young 'Lambic', and then leaving it to ferment in the bottle. The result is very spritzy, usually bottled with a champagne-style cork and wire, and is sometimes

called Champagne beer.
Drinkers often add a dash of
grenadine syrup to take the
edge off the sourness

harang – herring

hochepot – hotpot stew

homard – lobster

huîtres – oysters

huîtres à la gueuze – oysters in
sour beer

jambon d'Ardennes – cured ham
from the Ardennes

jets de Houblon – hop shoots

kip-kap – brawn made from
knuckle of ham or offal (pork
tongue, rind trotters and tail)
and set in aspic

Kriek – a sweet beer flavoured
with cherries

Lambic – a typically Bruxellois
beer, very old-fashioned,
made by an ancient technique
which only survives in
Belgium (and only in the area
around Brussels), made using
spontaneous fermentation
techniques

lapin à la kriek – rabbit braised
in cherry beer

lotte à la kriek – monkfish with
cherry beer

moules à l'escargot – a platter of
mussels grilled with garlic and
herb butter

moules-frites – a pot of mussels
served with chips

moules au vin blanc – a pot of
mussels cooked in white wine

moules marinière – a pot of
mussels cooked with celery,
onion and parsley

moules moutarde – a pot of
mussels cooked in a mustard
and cream sauce

moules poulette – a pot of
mussels cooked in a
mushroom, lemon and cream
sauce

moules provençale – a pot of
mussels cooked with tomatoes,
herbs and garlic

mousse au chocolat belge –
Belgian chocolate mousse

pain à la grecque – a caramelised
sugar biscuit

pintadeau à la framboise –
guinea fowl in raspberry beer

pistolet – a bread roll

plattekeis – soft white cheese
flavoured with chives – the
traditional accompaniment to
Lambic and Gueuze-type
beers. Also *ettekeis* – a sharp-
flavoured variation – or
pottekeis, a mixture of the
two. They are usually spread
on brown bread, then topped
with radishes and finely
chopped onion.

poire pochée – pear poached in
cherry beer

poulet à la Bruxelles – chicken
stuffed with cheese and basted
in beer

poussin à l'estragon – tarragon
spring chicken

praline – a term used in Belgium
for any filled chocolate
(containing cream, marzipan,
liqueur, etc)

raie au beurre noir – skate
cooked in black butter (with
capers and parsley)

ribbeke – pork spare ribs

rognons de veau à la Trappiste –
calves' kidneys in Trappist
beer

salade à l'ardennaise – salad with
strips of Ardennes ham

salade liégeoise – a warm salad
of green beans, new potatoes
and bacon pieces

saumon à la Hoegaarden –
salmon on caramelised
endives with white beer and
pistachio sauce

sole à la zeebrugeoise – sole with lobster sauce

soupe à la bière – beer soup

soupe de moules – mussels, cream and saffron soup

speculoos – a sweet caramelised biscuit, spiced with ginger, cinnamon, nutmeg and cloves

steak à l'américain – steak tartare with its own special seasoning

stoemp – mashed potatoes with mashed seasonal vegetables (leeks, endives, or other), usually served with sausages or bacon

tarte au citron – lemon tart

tarte au fromage – cheesecake

tarte aux fruits – fruit tart

tarte au riz – creamy rice tart

tarte au sucre – almond cream tart

tarte Tatin – upside-down caramelised apple and sponge pudding

toast cannibale – raw minced beer on toast

tomates farcies de crevettes grises – tomatoes stuffed with shrimps and mayonnaise

waterzooi à la gantoise – a stew of chicken and vegetables, cooked in a broth enriched with parsley, lemon and cream

waterzooi aux poissons – fish stew in a cream sauce

witbier – a light, refreshing, 'white beer' (also called *bière blanche*), made of wheat and customarily served with a slice of lemon

witloof au gratin – braised chicory wrapped in ham with a bechamel sauce, then gratinéed

zakouskis – a term used for any bite-sized snack

Recipes

Carbonnade flamande (Flemish beef stew)

This dish dates back to medieval times, when the beef was originally cooked with water, onions and thyme. Later, beer was substituted for water. Its earthy taste enhanced the beef, and it proved an excellent tenderiser for poor cuts of meat.

Serves 6

INGREDIENTS

4lb steak, cut into bite-sized pieces

2 tbsp flour

salt and pepper

4 tbsp unsalted butter

1oz brown sugar

1 tbsp freshly grated nutmeg

3 large onions thinly sliced

2 bottles of Belgian beer (preferably a rich, dark and slightly bitter one, such as Rodenbach, Abbey or Liefmans Goudenband)

2 tbsp tomato purée

2–3 springs of fresh thyme

2 bay leaves

1½ tbsp redcurrant jelly

1 tbsp cider or red wine vinegar

2 cooking apples

1. Season the beef cubes and coat in flour. Shake off any excess.
2. Melt 3 tbsp of butter in a large frying pan, add the beef, sugar and nutmeg, and sauté the meat until it is browned on all sides. Transfer it to a large saucepan.
3. Add the remaining butter and cook the onions until browned. (This helps to give the stew its deep brown colour.) Add them to the large saucepan.
4. Pour the beer into the pan and bring to the boil. Stir in the tomato purée and pour the mixture over the meat. Add the thyme and bay leaves.
5. Cover and simmer for 1½ to 2 hours over a low heat.
6. Before serving, remove the thyme and bay leaves, and stir in the redcurrant jelly and vinegar. Peel and quarter the apples, add to the casserole, and cook for a further 5 to 10 minutes, until the apple pieces are tender. This sweet-and-sour combination will enhance the authentic Flemish flavour.
7. Taste and adjust the seasoning.
8. Serve immediately with a generous dollop of *stoemp* (mashed potatoes and vegetables, *see page 26*).

Moules Marinière (Steamed mussels)

This is the simplest, tastiest and most common preparation for mussels. It is vital that the mussels are thoroughly cleaned before you cook them. Rinse them under cold water, scrubbing them with a brush to remove sand and seaweed, then use a small knife to scrape away the beard and any encrusted dirt. Then cook them as soon as possible after they are cleaned.

Serves 2

INGREDIENTS

3 tbsp unsalted butter

1 clove of garlic

2 large shallots or 1 medium onion, finely chopped

2 sticks celery, finely chopped

2kg mussels

1 tsp fresh thyme

1 bay leaf

2 tbsp fresh parsley, finely chopped

100ml dry white wine

freshly ground black pepper

1. Melt the butter in a large casserole pot. Add the garlic, shallots and celery and cook for about 5 minutes until the vegetables are softened but not browned.
2. Add the mussels, sprinkle with thyme and add the bay leaf, half the parsley and the black pepper. Add the white wine and cover the pot tightly.